Entangled Desires

A Tale of Love and Betrayal

TYREE WHITWORTH

Dedication

To everything in my past,

The experiences, challenges, and triumphs that have shaped me into who I am today.

You have made me realize that I am somebody worthy and capable of achieving my dreams.

To my beloved wife,

Your constant support and belief in me have been my greatest strength.

Thank you for standing by my side through every step of this journey.

To my godmother and sister, Zena,

Your faith in my abilities has inspired me to reach for the stars.

Your encouragement has been a beacon of light, guiding me towards success.

This book is a testament to the power of love, support, and the unyielding belief that we can accomplish anything we set our minds to.

Acknowledgments

Writing "Entangled Desires" has been a journey filled with many challenges and triumphs, and I could not have done it alone. I am deeply grateful to:

- My family: For their unwavering support and encouragement. For their patience and understanding as I poured my heart into this project.
- My editor, Chelsea: Your keen eye and insightful feedback have been invaluable.
- My beta readers: Thank you for your honest opinions and suggestions. Your input has been crucial in shaping this story.
- All the readers: Who have taken the time to explore this story. Your support means everything to me.

Lastly, a special thank you to my wife Chelsea, whose love and inspiration have been the backbone of this book. Your belief in me has made all the difference.

Foreword

When I first sat down to write "Entangled Desires," My plan was to create more than just a romance novel. I aimed to explore the depths of human emotions—the joys and sorrows, the love and betrayal that define our most intimate relationships.

This story was born out of a fascination with the complexities of love and hate, the way it can both uplift and entangle us. I have always believed that love is the greatest adventure, that can lead us to the highest peaks and the deepest valleys.

Through the characters of this book, I hope to take you on a journey that reflects the real-life struggles and triumphs of love. This book is a testament to the enduring power of passion and the resilience of the human heart.

This was written to inspire anyone who was ever told they could not do something or for anyone who has felt like they didn't matter to people. You do matter, and you can do anything you put your mind to.

Your past mistakes don't define who you are or who you're meant to be. What you do after past mistakes will define the person you're meant to be.

Thank you for choosing to read this story. I hope it resonates with you as much as it did with me while writing it.

Tyree Whitworth

Table of Contents

Prologue ....
Chapter 1...
Chapter 2...2
Chapter 3...3
Chapter 4...4
Chapter 5...6
Chapter 6...7
Chapter 7...8
Chapter 8...9
Chapter 9...10
Chapter 10 12
Chapter 11 13
Chapter 12 14
Epilogue...15

PROLOGUE

Books are not just about words; they transcend the literal, inviting readers to surrender to their imagination and immerse themselves in the realm of fantasy. The experience can be likened to a playground for the mind to immerse itself in worlds where imagination takes the reins.

They bring forth the power to stir emotions, spark desires, and unlock gateways to worlds unknown. Just as in life, literature, and even on the screen, the human heart yearns for the unattainable, craving the thrill of the unknown and the allure of what lies beyond reach. As destinies intertwine, the outcome remains unknown, like the pages of an unfinished story waiting to be written.

Books are more than the literal sum of their words; they beckon surrender and immersion into worlds where imagination unfurls its wings. In my lifetime, I have borne witness to the ceaseless human pursuit of the unattainable, be it within the realm of reality, the boundless pages of books, or even the flickering screens of television.

Fantasies and life's passions intermingle in a dance, with karma becoming permanently enmeshed – a narrative untold, much like the pages of an unfinished epic waiting to be filled with words of wonder.

Life is marked by aspirations that seem just out of reach, evoking an enduring yearning for the intangible. These yearnings remain akin to the blank pages of an unfinished story, waiting for the right words to be expressed. Within the vibrant backdrop of a bustling city, where dreams and reality coexist in an intricate dance, lives unfold like threads in a complex pattern, their fates entwined by the hands of fate.

The city becomes an arena where the human narrative takes center stage, dramas echoing in stories crafted by authors seeking to captivate hearts and minds. Amidst this dynamic backdrop, lives intersect, and narratives entwine, forming a web of relationships mirroring the plotlines of novels, where destinies converge in unexpected and captivating ways.

These unspoken cravings and longings in life mirror the untold possibilities within the unwritten sections of a story. Bonds are forged through shared experiences and trials, much like an intricate mosaic, woven by novelists whose characters' paths inevitably intersect.

Yet, behind the veil of unity, hidden motives and concealed truths lurk, reminiscent of the subtext that adds depth to a compelling tale.

Shared experiences and adversities forge bonds that mirror the relationships authors meticulously craft to bind their characters in unforeseen alliances, blurring the lines between loyalty and betrayal. Twists and turns alter a narrative's course, while these lives embark on a journey where loyalties fluctuate, allegiances shift, and alliances tremble.

As the chapters of time unfold, shadows deepen, and the mix of emotions and intentions becomes increasingly complex. Beneath the veneer of unity, lies a realm of concealed intentions and unvoiced realities, underlying accounts underneath the words of a captivating story. Themes of trust and disloyalty emerge, playing out in ways that are both heart-wrenching and captivating.

Desires, often cloaked in layers of confusion, steering their choices, blurring the fine line separating allegiance from deception. The outcome remains disguised in uncertainty, a suspenseful climax awaiting revelation, akin to the resolution of an unfinished narrative that beckons readers to unravel its secrets. Like the plot twists that transforms, their lives are embedded in a voyage where loyalties change, and commitments reposition like sand beneath shifting tides.

In the sprawling urban expanse, where aspirations collide with realities, the lives of individuals interlace, revealing a tale knitted from threads of dreams, ambitions, secrets, and the looming specter of treachery. With the passage of time, the chapters of their stories unfurl, shadows deepen, and the intricate tapestry of emotions and intentions becomes more labyrinthine.

Much like authors who possess the power to conjure redemption and forgiveness through their words, the lives intertwined within these intricate combinations embark on a journey of transformation. Themes of trust and betrayal surface, playing out in a symphony that evokes both heartache and fascination, much like the climaxes in masterful narratives.

Their paths promise the possibility of a conclusion that resolves the intricate threads of their existence. The finale remains uncertain, a suspenseful escalation yet to be disclosed, like the final resolution of an incomplete chronicle, inviting readers to unearth its concealed revelations.

With the passage of time, the chapters of their stories unfold, darkening the complexities of emotions and intentions become more twisted. Themes of trust and duplicity surface, playing out in a symphony that evokes both heartache and fascination, much like the climaxes in masterful narratives.

As expectations interlace and lives draw closer, their individual stories merge to form chapters within a grander saga. Unseen currents unite them, resembling characters destined to intersect within the elaborate blend of existence. An alliance, even though fragile, emerges, cemented by trust born of necessity and the shared trials of twisted fates. Yet, beneath the camaraderie's surface, seeds of betrayal lie dormant, awaiting the opportune moment to sow doubt and mistrust.

In the heart of the city, skyscrapers seem to touch the heavens and vibrant streets pulsate with life; the individual circumstances entwine. The lively streets harbor a tale that mirrors the complexities of human passions of the heart. Lives embarked on a dance of destiny that defied rational comprehension, inviting readers to explore its depths.

Threads of fate, invisible yet binding, wove their paths together with a deftness reminiscent of a master weaver crafting an enigmatic blackout. Little do they fathom that their shared journey will unravel, revealing a portrait interlaced not just with the threads of fate, but also interwoven with the piercing and painful strands of betrayal. Destinies continue to enmesh, and the ending lingered uncertainly, like the empty sheets of a book.

Their worlds, assorted and unalike, collide at unforeseen intersections, drawn closer by currents, like ships navigating an unrelenting tempest. Each person represents a distinct thread, and the pull of concealed currents draws them closer. Lurking beneath this camaraderie's façade, secrets festered like dormant wounds, slowly contaminating the air, and sowing insidious seeds of skepticism and mistrust.

A delicate alliance emerges, born out of necessity and survival, cemented by trust that appears unshakable. Yet, beneath the surface of their camaraderie, secrets fester like concealed wounds, subtly poisoning the air between them and planting the treacherous seeds of doubt and mistrust.

Threads of fate, unseen yet indelible, wove their trajectories together, entwining them in a puzzle that their stories became one. Unbeknownst to them, this shared journey would inevitably unravel, revealing a combination interlinked not just with destiny's threads but also the piercing shards of betrayal.

As the storm clouds gathered above, casting a shadow over the city, a final piece of the puzzle falls into place. The city whispered words that sent shivers down the spines of those gathered around her. "The threads of your lives are blended together, destined to cross and recross in the tapestry of fate. Each choice you make, each path you tread, will draw you closer, whether you seek it or not."

In that moment, the people who had been brought together by chance felt the invisible bonds of destiny tighten around them. They exchanged uneasy glances, recognizing the gravity of the words. The mysteries of their intertweaved destinies were beginning to unravel, and they knew they could not escape what lay ahead.

CHAPTER 1

As I stare out of the window, most guys my age are worrying about college applications, parties, and celebrating before adulthood comes knocking. But not me. Instead, I found myself sitting in a prison cell, imagining what life has in store for me.

Thinking about being in that cold, sterile courtroom, facing a judge who did not know me from Adam, stealing glances at the only family I had left, my older brother Edwin and his girlfriend and family friend Jessica. She sat beside him, offering me a sympathetic smile as the gavel came down. He was the golden boy, the star athlete, the one everyone in high school had adored. Jessica was the head cheerleader and the kindest person you would ever meet.

Thoughts of the promises said to me after being handed an eight-year sentence, which felt like a lifetime. They promised they would stay connected and be there for me. Never being in this situation before, I believed each one of them sitting in the courtroom, but as time crawled by behind bars, it became clear that only Jessica would stay true to her word.

She has always had a soft spot for me in her heart, seeing me as someone who is misunderstood and only wanted to stand out to his family due to his brother being the star athlete. I clung to the hope that my brother would eventually reach out. After all, we are blood. But months turned into years, and Edwin's absence from my life felt like a betrayal I could not forgive. Resentment festered, and I began to think of ways to get back at him. I wanted him to feel the isolation and abandonment I had endured.

In the beginning of my sentence, I spent my days in that dim, oppressive cell, running through countless scenarios in my mind. I thought about the texts I would never send, the phone calls I would never make, and the visits that would never happen. Edwin, with his sports star status and charismatic charm, had moved on from his awkward, misunderstood brother. The hurt and pain stung like a thousand cuts. But amidst the darkness, there was a flicker of light. Jessica remained a constant presence in my life. She wrote letters filled with stories about the outside world, about the small joys and sorrows that kept her going. She told me about her job, her dreams, and sometimes about the weather. Her words became my lifeline, a connection to a world I thought I had lost forever.

I could not help but feel a special place in Jessica's heart. It was her kindness, her unwavering support, which gave me the strength to keep going. As the days of my sentence dwindled down to mere months, I realized that while Edwin had turned his back on me, Jessica had remained an anchor. The past years have been a blur of bars and cold, harsh realities. I had lost touch with all of the little friends I had, and the world outside had moved on without me. Or, so I thought.

One afternoon, as I sat in my cell, I was handed an envelope during mail call. My heart skipped a beat, I thought it was another letter from Jessica, but when I saw the return address: Raphael Mitchell, my mind flashed back to those days of innocence before life got serious. Raphael was my best friend from elementary school, the friend I used to explore the streets of New York City with. He moved after both his parents passed away in a horrible car crash, that happened towards the end of the fifth grade. We were able to stay connected off and on over the years but once I started down the path that ended me here, I stopped reaching back out.

I tore open the envelope and unfolded the letter, my hands trembling. The words on the page danced before my eyes as I began to read:

"Hey Chaz,

I hope this letter finds you okay. I know it has been a long time, and I cannot believe it took me this long to find out what happened. When I moved back to the city a few years ago, I asked around about you, but no one would tell me anything. Until a few weeks ago, it was like you had disappeared.

I was walking down the street in the old neighborhood when I saw someone I recognized. It was your brother, Edwin. I could not believe my luck. I approached him, and at first, he did not recognize me. We talked, and he finally opened up about what happened to you.

Chaz, I could not believe it when Edwin told me you were in prison. It broke my heart. I know we did not stay in touch that often when I moved away, but I never imagined it would come to this. I am so sorry I was not there for you when you needed a friend the most.

I have spent the last few weeks learning about what you have been through, and I cannot even begin to imagine the challenges you have faced. I want you to know that I am here for you now, no matter what.

When you get out, I want to help you get back on your feet. We have a lot of catching up to do, and I cannot wait to hear your side of the story.

Stay strong, Chaz. The city has not been the same without you, and I cannot wait to welcome you home with open arms.

Your friend, Raphael"

Tears welled up in my eyes as I read Raphaels words. Some of the weight of seven long years seemed to lift from my shoulders. It meant the world to me that he had sought me out, that he wanted to be there for me despite everything. Even though I wish my brother would have reached out, especially since someone who I have not seen in years took the time to do so. The bitterness and resentment that had festered towards him began to deepen into that thin line between love and hate.

In those last few months of my sentence, I held onto Raphaels letter like a lifeline. It was a reminder that even when you think you have lost everything, sometimes old friends resurface just when you need them the most. With Raphaels support and the prospect of rekindling our friendship, I faced my impending release with a newfound sense of optimism and the belief that life after prison could still hold promise. Even if my brother is a heartless dick.

With less than 60 days left of my sentence, I am not the same person anyone used to know. These prison walls have reshaped me, both physically and mentally. I have gained muscle and covered myself in tattoos, marks of survival in a world I never thought I would find myself. It has been a dark and lonely road, but I am counting down the days until I can light the world on fire once I am released.

Today, I sat down in my cell with a pen in hand, ready to reply to a letter that had arrived a few days ago. The return address on the envelope read "Raphael Mitchell," and seeing his name brought a rush of emotions. Raphael was a long-lost friend, someone who had understood me like no one else. We were outsiders together, two kids who did not fit in.

I began my letter, my words flowing onto the paper like a long-awaited confession:

"Raphael,

It has been ages since I heard from you, and your letter was like a lifeline thrown into this dark abyss. I cannot tell you how much it means to hear from my old friend. It has been a crazy ride on this side of the bars, and I am not the same guy you used to know. These years have changed me, man, in more ways than I can explain.

I cannot help but wonder, has Edwin finally decided to write to me? I do not hold out much hope, though. It is like I never existed in his world, especially once I ended up here. I guess it is what I get for trying so hard to get our family to notice me, to be something more than just 'Edwin's brother.' I got tired of being misunderstood, of being the outcast.

You remember the last time we talked, right? I told you about Edwin's girlfriend, Jessica. God, she used to look so sexy back in high school, and I could not help but admire her from afar. Well, over the years, she has sent me photos, and I will tell you this—she looks a hell of a lot better now than she did back then. It is a mystery to me what she sees in that pretty boy. He does not even play sports anymore.

But enough about that. I have been thinking a lot about the world outside these prison walls. Once I am out, I am planning to find some women and have some fun. These years here have taught me that life's too short to hold back. I need to make up for lost time.

Raphael, You, and Jessica are the only two people who have understood me through all of this. Losing you when you moved away was like losing my right hand, the only person who shared my outsider perspective. I hope you have been well, and that life's been treating you better than it has treated me.

Stay in touch, my friend. Your letters are a lifeline in this bleak place.

Chaz"

As the days on my prison sentence dwindled down, my mind often drifted to what lay beyond those barbed-wire fences. I could not help but obsessively think about the life I was going to lead once I got out, especially when it came to women. It was like a wildfire, this longing, and it raged within me, fueled by years of isolation and envy.

There is something about incarceration that makes you crave freedom in its purest forms. I could not wait to feel the warmth of the sun on my skin, breathe the fresh, unfiltered air, and, most of all, be around women again. I had spent years behind these cold, unforgiving walls, and now, with freedom on the horizon, the possibilities seemed endless.

In my cell, I would lie awake at night, imagining the scenarios that awaited me. I thought about the women I might meet, the connections I would form, and the passions we would explore together. How I cannot wait to be able to explore a woman's body from top to bottom and front to back. Admiring the curves. waiting to run my tongue against her soft skin. Running my fingers over the goosebumps of her body. Feeling the dripping wet ocean between her legs. As well as her tight tonsil around my well-endowed cock.

It was a tantalizing dream, one that kept me going when despair threatened to swallow me whole.

Beneath this eagerness for the sensual pleasures of life, there was something darker, something that had been festering within me for years. It was the anger, the resentment, the bitterness I harbored toward my own flesh and blood—my brother, Edwin.

Edwin had always been the golden boy. The star athlete, the high school heartbeat, the one everyone admired. Meanwhile, I was the odd one out, the misunderstood sibling who could not live up to his shining legacy. I had spent years trying to prove myself, trying to get noticed, to make my mark. But instead, I had landed myself in this godforsaken prison.

The anger bubbled up like a volcano, simmering beneath the surface, threatening to erupt at any moment. Edwin's indifference, his complete disregard for my existence, fueled that rage. He acted as if I were a mere shadow, an inconvenient blemish on his otherwise perfect life. It was infuriating.

As I lay in my bunk, I could not help but hatch plan after plan for my brother. I envisioned ways to make him hurt the same way he had hurt me, to make him understand the pain of abandonment and neglect that had been my constant companion in this place. The more I thought about it, the more elaborate my schemes became.

I imagined taking everything he held dear and ripping it away, just as he had ripped me from his life. I dreamt of exposing his secrets, his weaknesses, and making sure the world saw him for the flawed human he was. I longed for the day when I could stand before him, victorious and unapologetic, as he finally recognized the brother he had forsaken.

But then, just when my anger reached its peak, a letter arrived. It was not from Edwin, as I had hoped in my darkest moments, but from someone unexpected—Jessica, Edwin's girlfriend.

Dear Chaz,

I hope this letter finds you well and brings some light to your days in there. I wanted to reach out and let you know about the conversations Edwin, and I have been having regarding your future.

Firstly, congratulations on your upcoming release! We are thrilled that you will soon have the opportunity to start anew. Edwin and I have been discussing the idea of you coming to stay with us once you are out. I know Edwin has some reservations, but I believe in giving family a chance.

Chaz, I have seen the changes in you over the years through your letters, and I genuinely believe you deserve a fresh start. We want to help you reintegrate into society, find a job, and rebuild your life. It will not be easy, but with support, it is possible.

Now, onto some personal news—I am excited to share that Edwin and I got engaged! We are embarking on a new chapter in our lives, and we would love for you to be a part of it. We are planning a small celebration, and it would mean the world to us if you could attend.

I understand if you have reservations about staying with us, but I hope you will consider our offer. Please let me know your thoughts and how you feel about the idea. We want to ensure your transition from prison goes as smoothly as possible.

Looking forward to hearing from you, Chaz. Stay strong and know that there are people who care about your future.

With love,

Jessica

She had reached out to me, and the contents of her letter were both surprising and confounding.

Jessica wrote about her and Edwin, about their life together since high school. She spoke of their shared dreams, and their deepening love. They got fuckin' engaged. But what struck me the most was her offer— a place to live when I got out of prison.

As I read her words, my mind raced. I could not believe it. Jessica, the woman I had secretly admired all those years ago, was reaching out to me, offering me shelter and support. It was a gesture of kindness I had not expected, and it left me conflicted. As well as ingenious!

With Jessica's letter in hand, I began to delve into the intricacies of her life with my brother. It was clear that they had built a world together, one that did not include me. Edwin had transformed from the high school sports star into a man who had found success in his career. They had a comfortable life, and Jessica had blossomed into a woman of elegance and grace.

Yet, as I read about their life together, I could not help but sense a growing tensity, particularly in Edwin's reaction to Jessica's offer to let me stay with them after my release. It was evident that he was not thrilled about the prospect of having me back in their lives.

Edwin had always been protective of his image, fiercely guarding the facade of perfection he had carefully crafted over the years. The thought of me reentering the picture, with my tattoos and the rough edges I had gained in prison, seemed to threaten his carefully constructed world.

I began to weigh my options. Jessica's offer was both a lifeline and a potential source of turmoil. On the one hand, it meant I would have a place to go when I got out and be around someone, I have a heartful of hatred for. On the other hand, I could sense the storm brewing between Jessica and Edwin, and I could use this to bring down his perfect world and exact my revenge.

As I counted down the days to my release, I could not escape the critical issues that plagued my mind. What had transpired between Jessica and Edwin during my absence? How had their relationship evolved, and why had Jessica reached out to me offering me a place to live? And, most importantly, how would my presence in their lives alter the delicate balance they had established?

In the end, I could not deny the allure of Jessica's offer. It was a chance to rebuild my life, to forge a connection with someone who had reached out to me when my own brother had turned his back. But the anger and resentment I felt toward Edwin remained, simmering beneath the surface like a dormant volcano, waiting for the right moment to erupt.

As the final days of my sentence approached, I knew that my reunion with Jessica and Edwin would be far from simple. It would be a collision of worlds, a test of boundaries, and a reckoning with the past. And as I prepared to step back into the world outside, I could not help but wonder if I was ready for the challenges and uncertainties that awaited me.

CHAPTER 2

Raphael stood in his small apartment, clutching his phone with the message he had received from Jessica, Edwin's fiancée. His brow was furrowed with confusion, and his mind raced as he tried to make sense of the message. It was an unusual situation, to say the least.

The apartment was bathed in the soft, golden light of the late afternoon sun, casting long shadows across the room. Raphael's fingers trembled slightly as he carefully opened the message.

"Raphael,

I hope this finds you well. It has been quite some time since we last had contact and I was told that you ran into and spoke with Edwin. You recently learned about Chaz's situation, and it prompted me to reach out to you."

Jessica's words jumped out at him, and he could not help but feel a sense of bewilderment. Why was Jessica writing to him instead of Edwin, knowing he had been his brother's longtime friend? Edwin and Jessica were practically inseparable, and Raphael could not recall a time when they had communicated separately until now, Chaz's release.

He continued reading, his eyes scanning the lines of the message.

"Chaz and I have been corresponding during his time in prison, and it has been an eye-opening experience. He has changed a lot over the years, and I believe he deserves a second chance at life. Despite everything, he is still Edwin's brother, and family is important."

Raphael's confusion deepened. Chaz, Edwin's brother, had been incarcerated for years, and the family had been distant throughout his ordeal. The fact that Jessica was reaching out to him and speaking about Chaz's changes left him feeling like there was a piece of the puzzle missing.

He took a deep breath and continued to read.

"I wanted to let you know that Edwin and I are offering Chaz a place to live once he is released from prison. I feel that he needs support and guidance during this crucial transition period. I know Edwin has some reservations, but I genuinely believe we can help Chaz get back on his feet."

Raphael could not help but wonder why Jessica was sharing this information with him. It was Edwin's family matter, and he could not comprehend why she would reach out to him instead of Edwin. It was all quite perplexing.

As he read on, Jessica's words continued to perplex him.

"Now, onto some personal news—I'm excited to share that Edwin and I got engaged! We are embarking on a new chapter in our lives, and we would love for you to be a part of it. We are planning a small celebration, and it would mean the world to us if you could attend.

We would love for you to be a part of our journey, in helping with him, Raphael.

I hope to hear from you soon. Please let me know your thoughts on Chaz coming to stay with us, and I would love to get together and talk about all that has been happening in your life.

Take care and stay safe.

Sincerely, Jessica"

Engaged? Raphael's eyes widened as he read the word. Chaz had not said anything about Edwin and Jessica getting engaged. The whole situation seemed surreal, like he had been thrust into a parallel universe where the pieces did not quite fit together.

Raphael closed the message and ran a hand through his beard. He needed to make sense of this situation, and he needed to do it quickly. Losing track of time, he realized he needed to rush to see Cassie, the devoted middle school teacher who had been a source of support and relaxation for him.

As he walked to surprise Cassie, his thoughts whirled. He could not shake the feeling that there was something more to Jessica's message, something that remained unspoken. He pondered whether Edwin was aware of her decision to reach out to him and invite Chaz into their lives.

Raphael could not help but wonder about the dynamics between Edwin and Jessica, the reservations Edwin had about Chaz staying with them, and how this engagement fit into the equation. He felt like an outsider, caught in a whirlwind of emotions and revelations that he could not quite grasp.

As he approached Cassie's school, he knew he had to put aside his bewildered thoughts for the moment and focus on the person who had been there for him when he needed it most. Cassie was a source of comfort and stability in his life, and he knew he could confide in her about the peculiar message from Jessica.

With each step, he braced himself for the upcoming conversation, hoping that Cassie might shed some light on this enigmatic situation and provide the clarity he so desperately needed.

Raphael strolled down the streets of New York City, a place that he had so many memories from childhood before the loss of his parents. He had a particular destination in mind today - the local middle school. It was a crisp autumn late afternoon, and Raphael had been looking forward to this visit for a while now.

Inside the school, he found himself in the hallways filled with the energy of pre-adolescent students coming from practice. He had come to meet an incredibly special person, Cassie, known for her exceptional rapport with her students.

Cassie was a petite woman 5'2 known as slim, thick. Her dress hugged her curves and the most perfect smile. With an unwavering commitment to her career, it made him want to take her even more. Her classroom was adorned with colorful posters, student artwork, and an inviting atmosphere that made learning fun. Middle schoolers could be a challenging bunch, but Cassie had an extraordinary way of connecting with them.

As Raphael entered her classroom, he found Cassie sitting at her desk, engrossed in grading papers. She looked up, her eyes lighting up as she saw him.

"Raphael!" Cassie exclaimed, rising from her chair. "It's so great to see you. What brings you here today?"

Raphael smiled and extended his arms to greet her with a big hug. Lifting her up off the ground "Cassie, it's always a pleasure. I wanted to surprise you and take you out to dinner."

After an intense day of grading papers and guiding her middle school students through various lessons, they chatted about the difficulties of teaching middle schoolers, and Cassie shared some of her recent success stories with Raphael. She was clearly passionate about her job, and it showed.

Cassie welcomed the prospect of a peaceful evening. She had spent hours poring over the assignments, leaving her feeling both accomplished and in need of a break.

As the final papers were carefully tucked into her bag, Cassie sighed with relief, knowing that the weekend lay ahead, offering a well-deserved respite. Her thoughts wandered to Raphael, a relaxation she had grown close to over the years.

Raphael, an artist with a fondness for bringing color and creativity into her life, had invited her to dinner that evening. It was a delightful prospect, a chance to unwind, enjoy good company, and forget about the stacks of papers for a while.

When they arrived at the charming Italian restaurant Raphael had chosen, they were greeted by the warm ambiance of the soft glow of candlelight flickered on the table and the scent of delicious cuisine creating an ambiance of warmth and intimacy. The host walked them over to their secluded reserved table.

Before they sat down, he greeted her with a gentle kiss on the cheek. " I forgot to tell you how lovely you look, as always."

Cassie's cheeks flushed with a soft shade of pink as she returned his smile. "Thank you, Raphael. You always know what to say to make me blush."

They settled into their seats, the cozy atmosphere of the restaurant wrapping around them like a comfortable embrace. Raphael had been eager to catch up with Cassie, to share his bewildering experience of receiving a message from Jessica, Edwin's fiancée, instead of Edwin himself. As they pursued the menu, he could not help but broach the subject.

"Cassie," he began, his voice laced with curiosity, "I can't get this message from Jessica out of my mind. I just can't wrap my head around it."

Cassie, her eyes reflecting the soft candlelight, nodded in understanding. "I can imagine it's quite perplexing, Raphael. What did she say, exactly?"

Raphael recounted the contents of the message, detailing Jessica's message about offering Chaz, Edwin's brother, a place to live upon his release from prison. He mentioned Edwin's reservations and Jessica's belief in giving Chaz a second chance.

Cassie listened attentively, sipping her wine as she processed the information. "It's a rather unusual situation," she mused, her fingers tracing the rim of her glass. "But perhaps Jessica reached out to you because she knew you could offer some insight into Chaz's past or provide support during his transition."

Raphael's brow furrowed. "But why not Edwin? Why didn't she discuss this with him? They're practically inseparable, and this involves his own brother."

Cassie leaned in slightly, her gaze thoughtful. "Sometimes, Raphael, it's easier to confide in someone outside the immediate family, especially when it comes to delicate matters. Maybe Jessica thought you could provide an outsider's perspective without the emotional baggage."

Raphael nodded, considering Cassie's words. It made sense, to a degree. Edwin and Jessica's relationship was undoubtedly strong, and perhaps Jessica wanted to handle the situation discreetly to avoid straining their relationship.

"Raphael you should not think too much into it and just be excited that Chaz is about to come home. "That's wonderful news!" Cassie exclaimed.

Raphael nodded. "Yes, it is great news, but something out of this whole situation just doesn't sit right in my gut and she mentioned that Edwin isn't entirely thrilled about the idea of Chaz staying with them. It seems like there might be some discomfort there."

Cassie's brow furrowed in concern. "That's not good. Chaz needs a stable environment to help him reintegrate into society. Edwin should be more supportive."

Raphael sighed. "I agree, and I think that's what Jessica is trying to provide. But she also mentioned that Chaz has changed a lot during his time in prison, and she's unsure of how it might affect their dynamic."

Cassie leaned back in her chair, deep in thought. "Chaz has had a difficult journey, and it's understandable that he's changed. I hope they can work things out."

As they continued to discuss Chaz's situation, Raphael noticed a hint of sadness in Cassie's eyes. He could not help but wonder if there was something more to her concern for Chaz than just a teacher's empathy.

Unbeknownst to Raphael, Cassie had been harboring a secret. It was a secret that she had kept locked away in the depths of her heart, hidden from everyone, even her closest friends.

During her high school years, long before Chaz had found himself in prison, Cassie had fallen deeply in love with him. She had admired him from afar, watching him navigate the complexities of teenage life with a quiet strength and determination. She had never found the courage to confess her feelings, and over time, they had drifted apart.

Despite the years that had passed since high school, Cassie's love for Chaz had never wavered. In fact, it had only grown stronger as she followed his journey from a distance. She had been secretly writing letters to him throughout his time in prison, pouring her heart out on paper, sharing her hopes, dreams, and firm support.

One evening, as the sun dipped below the horizon and the prison's cold walls seemed to close in on him, Chaz received a letter that was different from the others. It was from Cassidy, and it bore the weight of her deepest secret.

Their conversation about the perplexing message continued throughout dinner, as they shared their thoughts and speculations. As the evening wore on and their plates were cleared away, the mood shifted, and Raphael found himself drawn into Cassie's eyes.

With glasses of wine in hand, they retreated to a more intimate conversation. The low hum of conversations around them created a cocoon of privacy as they leaned in closer to each other.

Raphael's voice lowered, taking on a more seductive tone. "You know, Cassie, I couldn't help but notice how you always look so stunning."

Cassie's cheeks flushed as she met Raphael's gaze, her eyes filled with a mix of anticipation and want. "And you, Raphael, have a way of making a woman feel special."

Their fingers brushed against each other, sending shivers down their spines. The connection between them had always been strong, but tonight it felt charged with an irresistible tension.

As the night wore on, their conversation turned decidedly more sensual. Raphael leaned in, his lips brushing against Cassie's ear as he whispered, "I can't stop thinking about you."

Cassie's breath hitched, and she leaned in closer, her lips barely grazing his as she replied, "I've been wanting this all night."

Their kisses were slow and deliberate, each one building the intensity of their longing. Raphael's hands traced the contours of Cassie's body, sending waves of pleasure coursing through her. She felt herself soaking her panties. Their wine-soaked conversation had ignited a fire within them, and they could not resist the magnetic pull drawing them closer.

The night unfolded like a passionate symphony, each touch and kiss fueling their longing. They indulged in each other's fantasies, whispered their deepest desires, and surrendered to the electric chemistry that had always simmered beneath the surface.

As the restaurant began to empty, Raphael and Cassie knew they could not wait any longer. Their connection, forged through years of friendship, relaxation, and shared moments, had reached a point of no return.

Their lips met once more, this time in a searing, hungry kiss that left them breathless. Their fingers entwined as they made their way to Raphael's apartment, their bodies aching with anticipation.

As the door closed behind them, their longing burned brighter, Raphael pushed her forward pinning her against the wall, wrist above her head. Towering over her 5'2 demeanor, He whispered in her ear "I have been waiting all night for this." Grabbing both wrists with one hand he unzipped her dress from the neck down to her thick curvy behind. Allowing her arms to fall the dress slowly fell between the creases of her legs. Looking down he noticed that the only thing she wore underneath was her soft skin.

She whispers "I took my soaked panties off back in the restaurant's bathroom. Every time you touched my body the seat would feel increasingly like I was walking further and further into a pool." Their voices were a symphony of passion that filled the night.

Raphael turned her around, back against the wall. The moon shining through the window revealed her round breast and caramel nipple. He gently used his full lips to kiss from her neck to her lips. With one hand against the wall, his right hand touching the waterfall between her thick thighs. She slowly unbuttons his shirt, letting it fall onto the floor.

Rubbing her hands around his athletically defined chest.

During their passionate kissing Raphael unbuttons his pants. Allowing everything to fall, divulging his hard well-endowed erection. Lifting her up, she wraps her legs around him; he carries her to his room. While doing so, she gasps from his hard sex rubbing against the ocean between her legs. Raphael lays her onto the bed kneeling onto the floor. He raises her legs over his shoulders, ready to taste her juices. She grasps for breath from the overwhelming emotions rushing through her body.

Cassie's hands clinching the back of his neck from the sensation of his tongue against her sensitive clit. He climbs onto the bed, his left hand on her supple breast. He mounted her, legs already parted showing the inner flesh of her soft, thick thighs. Their bodies begging for what they know is about to come.

He thrust his cock deep inside of her, permitting her to feel every inch. With his left arm underneath, her, Raphael holds her firm in his grip. As he strokes slow and steady, he whispers in her ear "after tonight I'm going to own every part of your body." She sucked on his bottom lip allowing his body to pull the life out of her.

As they continued to explore each other's bodies, they realized that sometimes, the most intense connections could be found where you least expected them.

Hours passed in a whirlwind of pleasure, and as dawn broke, Raphael and Cassie lay intertwined in each other's arms, their bodies glistening with the aftermath of their raw emotions. Cassie's mind wonders about the secret that she has been keeping from Raphael about her knowing Chaz and even more that she has been in love with him since high school.

With whispered promises of more secret rendezvous and shared moments to come, they drifted into a contented slumber, knowing that the next part of their lives held a promise of secrets, excitement, and exploration they could not resist.

CHAPTER 3

As the first rays of dawn filtered through the curtains, Cassie stirred in the unfamiliar surroundings of Raphael's apartment. Memories of the previous night flooded her mind, a tapestry woven with laughter, shared secrets, and a connection she had not felt in years. The aroma of their dinner lingered in the air, a reminder of the exquisite meal they had shared before retiring to the intimacy of Raphael's home.

Whispered promises hung in the air like delicate threads, binding them together in a web of anticipation and desire. In the quiet moments before consciousness fully claimed her, Cassie reveled in the prospect of more clandestine rendezvous with Raphael to come, each one promising new adventures and shared moments that ignited her soul.

Fully awake now, reality set in, and Cassie's thoughts shifted to Chaz and his imminent release from prison. The joy of the previous night was tinged with a qualm of regret. She had allowed herself to be swept away by temptation, forgetting for a moment the complexities of her life and the responsibilities that awaited her. Rising from the bed to find her clothes, Raphael turned over and playfully slapped her ass, murmuring a cheerful, "Good morning."

Turning to face him, all she could see was the imprint of his hard, cut body and the imprint of his erect cock. He grabbed her hand, attempting to pull her back into bed. "What's wrong? Did you not enjoy yourself last night?" he asked, his voice filled with genuine concern.

With hesitation, Cassie replied, "I did, but do you see the time? I have to get up and going. I have no clothes here, I have to head to the gym, and I need to shower."

"You don't need a gym when you have me," Raphael responded with a playful grin. "I believe I'm enough of a workout from what we did last night. You can shower after, and you can wear some of my clothes. I thought we could enjoy a day in each other's company. You've had a long week at work and need a day to relax."

Cassie paused, considering his plan. The idea of spending the day in Raphael's company was tempting. She had indeed had a long week, filled with the usual stresses of work and the mounting anticipation of Chaz's return. A day of relaxation sounded perfect, yet the weight of her responsibilities pressed down on her.

"Raphael, it's not that I don't want to spend time with you," she began, choosing her words carefully. "But there are things I need to take care of, and I can't ignore them."

Raphael's expression softened with understanding. "I get it, Cassie. Life's complicated, and we all have our obligations. But just for today, let's take a break from all that. You deserve it."

Cassie sighed, feeling the stress between her pleasures and her duties. The lure of a day spent in Raphael's embrace was strong, but so were the demands of her life. She knew she had to find a balance, but in that moment, she was unsure how.

Reluctantly, Cassie agreed to stay a little longer. She slipped back into bed, nestling against Raphael's warm body. As they lay together, the morning light casting gentle shadows around the room, Cassie allowed herself to relax, if only for a while.

Throughout the day, Raphael made good on his promise to help her unwind. With his arms around her she swung her arm behind her back to grab his cock which was against her soft ass. He slide down the bed just a little bit so that his cock slid out of her hand. With one hand he grabbed his erection and with his other arm he grabbed both of her arms behind her back. He bent her over and slid inside her allowing her to feel every inch of him as he slowly allowed himself deeper and deeper. With the hand that was holding his erection he grabs her throat bringing it back towards him arching her back in the process giving himself more leverage to go deeper into the tight ocean between her luscious thick thighs.

With every thrust he whispers into her ear, "Now aren't you happy you stayed and spent the day relaxing with me."

"Yesssss!" She responds with a soft moan from all the sensations her body is feeling.

"Whose pussy is this?" he asked.

With all the excitement and vibrations that her body was feeling she answered "Yours daddy! All yours! Don't stop. Keeping going!"

As she started throwing her ass back against his dick, she felt his body about to climax. Abruptly pulling herself off of him.

With her hands on his chest, Cassie gently pushed Raphael flat onto the bed. His arousal stood prominently. She began kissing her way down from his chest, her full lips trailing over his skin, until she reached his manhood. She wrapped her lips around the tender head, her tongue swirling around the tip, teasing him. Inch by inch, she took him deeper, her throat accommodating his entire length.

Raphael was already sensitive, and Cassie's expert mouth work brought him quickly to the brink. In just minutes, he exploded, releasing into the back of her throat. Cassie swallowed every drop, savoring the moment before finally releasing him, leaving both of them breathless and satisfied.

While they were catching their breath she decided to lounge around a little more with Raphael, laughing, watching movies, sharing stories, chatting, and enjoying each other's company, as if the world outside didn't exist. He cooked them a delicious breakfast, and they ate together. Raphael's easygoing nature made it easy for Cassie to forget her worries, if only temporarily.

In those moments, Cassie felt a rare sense of peace. She knew that the complications of her life would return soon enough, but for now, she was content to live in the present, savoring the connection she had with Raphael. The day passed in a blissful haze, each moment a precious escape from reality.

As evening approached, Cassie knew she couldn't stay any longer. She needed to face the world outside and the responsibilities waiting for her. She reluctantly got dressed, wearing one of Raphael's shirts that smelled faintly of him. As she gathered her things, Raphael watched her with a mix of affection and understanding.

"I wish you could stay longer," he said softly, pulling her into a gentle embrace.

"I wish I could too," Cassie replied, her voice tinged with sadness. "But I have to go. There's so much I need to do."

Raphael nodded, his grip tightening around her for a brief moment before he let her go. "I understand. Just know that I'm here for you, whenever you need me."

Cassie smiled, grateful for his support. "Thank you, Raphael. I'll see you soon."

With a final kiss, she left his apartment, stepping back into the reality of her life. The streets were bustling with activity, a stark contrast to the serene cocoon she had shared with Raphael. As she made her way home, her mind raced with thoughts of Chaz and the complexities of her relationships.

Cassie knew she needed to figure out her feelings and decide what she wanted. Chaz's impending return added another layer of uncertainty to her life, and she could not ignore the fact that her heart was pulled in different directions. The time spent with Raphael had shown her that she was capable of feeling deep, passionate connections, but she needed to understand where those feelings fit into the bigger picture of her life.

Once home, Cassie took a long, hot shower, letting the water wash away the remnants of the day. She dressed in comfortable clothes and settled on her couch, a cup of tea in one hand and her phone in the other. She sent a text to her friend Vanessa saying, "We need to meet for coffee soon, let me know when is good I have a lot to tell you and pick your brain about." The evening stretched before her, a quiet contrast to the whirlwind of emotions she had experienced over the past 24 hours.

As she sipped her tea, Cassie reflected on her relationship with Vanessa since grade school. Vanessa had always been a source of wisdom and support, and Cassie knew she needed her friend's guidance now more than ever. The response was almost immediate, with Vanessa suggesting they meet at their favorite café. Cassie felt a sense of relief, knowing that she would soon have a chance to talk through her feelings with someone who understood her.

While sitting there, feeling relieved that she would soon be able to speak to Vanessa, Cassie flipped through the mail. She struggled to catch her breath at the sight of a responding letter from Chaz. Rehashing the letter she had sent him weeks before, she remembered pouring her heart out, telling him a lot of things, but the main point was that she had been in love with him from the first day she saw him because he was his own person and didn't follow crowd trends like everyone else.

With trembling hands, she opened the letter and began to read Chaz's response:

Dear Cassie,

This is a surprise to hear that you have been in love with me for all this time, why are you just now telling me? You should have told me this in one of the many letters from before. I have been in this place by myself for the most part with no connection to the outside world.

Being here has been a solitary experience. Most of my days are spent trying to keep to myself and avoid trouble. The guards and inmates here can be brutal, and it is a constant challenge to stay out of harm's way. I've had to build walls around myself. Both physically and emotionally, to survive. It's hard to trust anyone in here, and that isolation can really mess with your mind.

Your letters are like a ray of light in this dark place. It reminded me of who I was before all of this. The fact that you saw something in me that others didn't mean more than you can imagine. But it also brings up so many questions.

With you telling me that you have been in love with me. Where does that leave us with the fact that I come out very soon? What are we supposed to do with these feelings? I've thought a lot about the future, but it's always been so uncertain. And now. Knowing that you're waiting for me out there gives me hope but also makes me anxious.

I have to admit that I have changed. Prison does that to you. It's made me harder, more wary of the world. But this letter gives me a reason to believe that maybe. Just maybe. Theres a chance for me to find a piece of my old self again.

I need to know what you're expecting from me, Cassie. Are you ready to deal with the reality of who I've become? Can you see a future for us despite everything? I want to believe in something good, but I need to understand where we stand.

Yours sincerely,

Chaz

Cassie reread the letter several times, her emotions swirling in a storm of confusion and anticipation. She had not expected Chaz to respond so openly, and now she had to grapple with the implications of his words. Where did this leave them? What did it mean for her relationships with both Chaz and Raphael?

Feeling overwhelmed, Cassie decided to take a moment to center herself. She took deep breaths, trying to calm her racing thoughts. The questions Chaz raised were ones she had to answer, but she needed to sort through her feelings first.

As she lay in bed, Cassie's mind continued to whirl with thoughts of Chaz, Raphael, and the future. She knew she had to find clarity, to understand what her heart genuinely wanted. The prospect of seeing Vanessa the next day provided a glimmer of hope. Vanessa had always been her rock, the person who could help her make sense of her tangled emotions.

With that comforting thought, Cassie finally felt her mind quieting. She closed her eyes and let sleep take her, knowing that tomorrow would bring the much-needed conversation with Vanessa. It was time to confront her feelings and find the path that would lead her to happiness.

CHAPTER 4

Vanessa sat in a cozy café, her hands wrapped around a steaming mug of coffee, the warmth seeping into her palms as she waited for Cassie to arrive. The café, with its soft lighting and gentle hum of conversation, provided a comforting backdrop to Vanessa's anticipation. She glanced at the door periodically, her thoughts drifting to the whirlwind of recent events.

Just moments later, Cassie walked through the door, her presence immediately filling the room with energy. She made her way to Vanessa's table, her eyes sparkling with excitement. The moment she sat down, she launched into a vivid account of Raphael, a man who seemed to embody a fascinating blend of strength and vulnerability. Cassies animated gestures painted a picture of a man who was as imposing as he was intriguing.

Raphael stood at an impressive height of 6 feet 3 inches, his athletic build and striking bald head making him hard to miss. His full beard added to his commanding presence. Yet, despite his outward strength, Cassie revealed that he carried a deep sense of vulnerability. His past, marred by abandonment and loss, had left him with scars that were not immediately visible. Vanessa listened intently as Cassie described how Raphael's unstable childhood had instilled in him an unshakable fear of commitment. His stoic demeanor often masked the raw emotions that simmered beneath the surface.

As Cassie recounted her feelings about the previous night with Raphael, Vanessa noticed the mix of emotions playing across her friend's face. Cassie's voice wavered slightly as she admitted, "With Chaz coming home soon, this was a very unexpected event with Raphael. We have been friends for some time now and nothing has ever happened. I am not sure what to do!"

Vanessa leaned forward, her expression thoughtful. "You are a single woman, and the fact that Chaz is coming home does not change that. You spilling your emotions to him in a letter just happened, and you do not know how he feels. Especially since he has been locked up all this time, he might just want to come home and enjoy his freedom."

Cassie sighed, the weight of her predicament evident in her eyes. "But what about the fact that Chaz and Raphael know each other? Should I let them know about one another?"

Vanessa took a moment to consider this. She wanted to give Cassie the best advice she could. "Do not say anything quite yet. Enjoy your time with Raphael. Given his rough past, I promise you he will understand that you do not want to rush into anything and want to keep things casual between you two."

As Vanessa offered her counsel, her mind began to wander. The description Cassie had provided of Raphael—a 6'3" bald man with a sculpted body—sounded like the kind of man she would not mind having some fun with. She could not help but think about the possibilities. If Cassie intended to keep things casual with Raphael, why couldn't she entertain the idea of some fun too?

It had been three long years since Vanessa had any sexual contact with anyone. The last person had been a married man who frequented her place of business for a drink whenever he was in town. Their brief, passionate encounters had been a welcome distraction, but he had stopped coming by after his wife had their child. Since then, Vanessa's life had been a desert of intimacy, and the thought of a man like Raphael stirred something within her.

As Vanessa sat back in her seat, she could not shake the image of Raphael from her mind. She wondered what it would be like to feel his strong arms around her, to explore the depth of the vulnerability Cassie had described. The café's cozy atmosphere seemed to close in around her, making her more aware of her own desires and the possibilities that lay ahead.

Cassie continued to talk about her dilemma, her voice a mix of concern and hope. Vanessa offered her support, but her mind kept drifting back to Raphael. She felt a twinge of guilt for entertaining such thoughts, knowing how much Cassie was struggling with her feelings. Yet, she couldn't deny the excitement that Raphael's description had ignited within her.

As the conversation wound down, Vanessa and Cassie sat in companionable silence for a moment. Vanessa reached across the table and squeezed Cassie's hand. "Whatever you decide, I'm here for you," she said softly.

Cassie smiled, gratitude shining in her eyes. "Thanks, Vanessa. I really appreciate it."

In the end, Vanessa knew that life was unpredictable. But sitting in that cozy café, with the scent of coffee in the air and the warmth of friendship surrounding her, she felt ready to embrace whatever came her way. Whether it was a rekindled connection with an old flame or the thrill of a new adventure with Raphael, Vanessa was determined to live her life with an open heart and an adventurous spirit.

As they left the café, Vanessa couldn't help but feel a sense of anticipation. The future was uncertain, but it was also full of possibilities. She hoped that Cassie would find the clarity she needed, and perhaps, in the process, Vanessa might find a bit of excitement and adventure for herself. The thought of Raphael lingered in her mind; a tantalizing possibility that made her pulse quicken.

In the days that followed, Vanessa found herself thinking increasingly about Raphael. She wondered if their paths would ever be crossed, and if they did, what might happen. She felt a renewed sense of hope, a spark that had been missing for too long. As she navigated her own emotions and desires, she remained a steadfast friend to Cassie, offering support and understanding as they both faced the complexities of their hearts.

Weeks passed, and Chaz was finally released from prison. On his first day of freedom, Raphael planned to make the most of this special occasion. Throughout the evening, Raphael noticed Chaz frequently texting on his phone, trying to get Jessica, Edwin, and a few other people to join them. Unfortunately, everyone else was either working or otherwise occupied, leaving Chaz and Raphael to enjoy the night on their own.

Determined to make the most of it, Chaz and Raphael decided to embrace the spontaneity of the night. They set out with a loose plan: hop from one lounge and bar to another, enjoying each stop along the way, until Chaz met someone interesting. Couch Lounge was just the first of many stops they had in mind.

The energy at Couch Lounge was vibrant, and it didn't take long for Chaz to loosen up and start enjoying himself. Raphael, always the supportive friend, made sure Chaz had everything he needed to feel at ease. They reminisced about old times, shared laughter, and toasted to new beginnings. The mood was light, and the atmosphere electric with the buzz of conversations and the rhythm of the music.

While waiting at the bar, a young lady approached Raphael, noticing he hadn't been helped.

She asked, "How is everything? Can I get you something?"

He responded, "Just waiting for the bartender to order a drink. My friend is celebrating his first day home."

She replied, "Nice, congratulations! The first round is on me." Despite Raphael's protests, she insisted. Unbeknownst to Vanessa, Raphael was the man Cassie had been confiding to her about. As they talked, unaware of their interconnected pasts, Raphael shared his career stories, while Vanessa recounted her journey from teen event planner to Couch Lounge owner.

Vanessa had always been dedicated to her work, leaving little room for romance. But when she met this guy, his presence began to unravel her carefully constructed walls. The primal yearning he awakened within her was both exciting and terrifying. Vanessa found herself torn between her ambitions and desires, seeking guidance from Cassie, unaware of Cassie's connection to Raphael.

Vanessa's journey from teen event planner to successful entrepreneur had been one of hard work and little play. She had built multiple businesses and managed many employees, with success being her primary focus. But meeting him, a charming man that has his life together, changed everything. It had been years since Vanessa had been touched intimately, but Raphael's aura made her whole-body clench with desire. Their first conversation left her fantasizing about his touch, and she realized just how much she craved physical intimacy.

Vanessa and Raphael had agreed to keep their encounter spontaneous and exciting by exchanging numbers but not names. Vanessa entered her name as "Beautiful Lounge Owner" in his phone, and he saved his as "6 foot 3." The thrill of their interaction left Vanessa in a state of breathless anticipation. As she rushed to her office, she could feel the adrenaline coursing through her body, leaving her panties damp with excitement. The day passed in a blur of daydreams about Raphael's strong hands on her body, and her employees couldn't help but notice her distraction, casting curious glances and wondering if everything was okay.

Feeling both exhilarated and confused, Vanessa decided to reach out to her best friend Cassie. "Cassie, you won't believe what happened," she began, her voice a mix of excitement and confusion. Cassie listened attentively as Vanessa recounted her encounter with the mysterious "6 foot 3."

"That sounds amazing, Vanessa! I'm so happy for you," Cassie replied, genuinely thrilled for her friend. However, a small part of her was curious about the man who had captured Vanessa's attention.

Little did Casie know they are both talking to the same man. Vanessa trusted Cassie with all her secrets, never suspecting the coincidence that was about to unfold.

In their school days, Vanessa, Cassie, Chaz, and Raphael had all been classmates. However, Raphael's life took a tragic turn when his parents died in a car accident. The sudden loss left him devastated and alone, thrusting him into the foster care system. His journey through foster care led him to a Jamaican family in a different state, a situation that only intensified his sense of being an outsider. The cultural shift and the unfamiliar environment made it difficult for Raphael to adjust, adding layers of complexity to his already disorderly life.

Despite his challenging circumstances, Raphael always had his loyal friend in Chaz. Chaz was a constant source of support, always there to lend a helping hand or a listening ear. Their friendship provided Raphael with a sense of stability and belonging, even as the world around him felt increasingly uncertain. The bond between them was strong, built on mutual respect and shared experiences.

With Raphael unfortune move at the end of the 5th grade school year, meant losing touch with the few friends he had. The transition was jarring, uprooting Raphael from the familiar and thrusting him into yet another new environment. The separation was painful, marking the end of a significant chapter in his life.

In his new state, Raphael struggled to find his footing. The family he lived with was kind and welcoming, but the sense of displacement lingered. He missed the familiarity of his old school, the camaraderie of his friends, and the comfort of his routines. The weight of his parents' death and the constant changes in his life bore heavily on him, shaping his outlook and resilience.

Meanwhile, back in their original school, Vanessa and Cassie continued with their lives, unaware of Raphael's whereabouts. They often wondered what had happened to their friend, reminiscing about the times they had spent together. Vanessa, in particular, felt a pang of sadness whenever she thought of Raphael, wishing she could reach out to him somehow.

As the years went by, Raphael adapted to his new life as best as he could. He focused on his studies and eventually discovered a passion for acting and modeling. This newfound interest became an outlet for his emotions, allowing him to channel his experiences into his performances. His talent didn't go unnoticed, and he slowly began to build a name for himself in the industry.

Raphael returned to the excited Chaz, and they agreed to finish this drink and move on. As they moved from one place to another, their spirits remained high. Each bar and lounge offered a new adventure, a new set of faces, and a fresh chance for

Chaz to meet someone who could make his night even more memorable. Raphael kept an eye on his friend, noting how Chaz's demeanor shifted from cautious optimism to genuine enjoyment as the night wore on.

At one of the bars, Chaz struck up a conversation with a woman who seemed to match his energy perfectly. She stood at 4 feet 11 inches, a striking contrast to Chaz's towering 6-foot height. Her light-skinned complexion glowed under the bar's ambient lighting, highlighting her delicate features. She had an hourglass figure, accentuated by a fitted dress that showcased her curves with elegance. Her dark, curly hair framed her face, cascading down her back in loose waves. Her eyes sparkled with mischief and warmth, drawing people in with their intensity.

Meanwhile, Raphael found himself enjoying the night in his own way. He chatted with a few people, sipped his Smugglers Rhum on the Rocks, and soaked in the lively ambiance. It was a stark contrast to the quiet life he'd known growing up, but it felt good to be out, celebrating Chaz's return.

As the night progressed, Chaz and the woman he'd met seemed to be hitting it off. They moved closer, their conversation growing more animated. Raphael decided to give them some space, stepping outside for a breath of fresh air. He reflected on the journey that had brought them all to this point—Chaz's time in prison, his own struggles with displacement and loss, the night with Cassie and this mystery woman who owns the lounge.

Returning inside, Raphael saw Chaz smiling more than he had in years. It was clear that tonight was exactly what Chaz needed. They had managed to turn a simple plan into a memorable night of freedom and fun. The bond between them felt stronger, forged in the fires of their shared past and the excitement of the present.

As the night ended, Raphael, Chaz and his lady companion made their way back to Couch Lounge, where it had all started. As they walked in, the familiar ambiance brought a sense of nostalgia to Raphael. It was then that he noticed the owner behind the bar, her eyes lighting up when she saw him.

"Hey, 6 foot 3," Vanessa greeted him with a playful smile. Raphael chuckled, appreciating the light-hearted banter. They talked for a while, sharing stories, and laughing, completely unaware of the connections that surrounded them.

As the night went on, Raphael felt a growing sense of familiarity with Vanessa, though he could not quite place it. In a city of 8 million people in it how coincidental that would be.

Meanwhile, Vanessa was drawn to his magnetic presence, her curiosity about his past piqued. Their conversation flowed effortlessly, bridging the gap between their present selves and the shadows of their shared history.

Raphael returned to Chaz and his company, and they shared a final drink, toasting to friendship, freedom, and the promise of new beginnings. For Chaz, it was a night to remember, a symbol of his return to the world and the start of a new chapter. And for Raphael, it was a reminder of the enduring power of friendship and the unpredictable paths life can take.

CHAPTER 5

Chaz woke up, his mind hazy and disoriented. As he opened his eyes, he found himself lying next to the girl from the night before. Her presence brought a fleeting memory of laughter, dancing, and an undeniable chemistry. Glancing around the unfamiliar room, he realized he had no idea where he was. Panic set in briefly, but he quickly collected himself. He gently extricated himself from the bed, careful not to wake her, and grabbed his phone from the nightstand. He needed to get to Raphael's apartment and figure out his next move.

Chaz decided to stay with Raphael since his release, avoiding making any commitments about moving in with his future sister-in-law, Jessica, and his brother, Edwin. He hadn't given them a definitive answer, feeling the need to first get his bearings and decide what direction his life should take. Raphael's place had become a sanctuary for him, a space where he could think without pressure.

After dressing quietly, Chaz slipped out of the room and made his way outside, the crisp morning air a welcome relief from the stuffy apartment. He checked his phone and saw a few missed calls from Raphael, likely checking on his whereabouts. Chaz called a rideshare and soon found himself in route to Raphael's apartment.

When he arrived, Raphael was just heading out the door, looking fresh and ready for the day. He greeted Chaz with a knowing smile. "Rough night, huh?"

Chaz grinned sheepishly. "You could say that."

"I'm heading to a meeting," Raphael said. "Make yourself comfortable. Use the day to recuperate from last night's festivities. There's food in the fridge, and the TV remote is on the coffee table."

"Thanks, man. I appreciate it," Chaz replied, grateful for Raphael's understanding and hospitality.

Raphael's apartment was small but cozy, the kind of place that felt lived-in and welcoming. Chaz sank into the couch, the soft cushions offering a much-needed comfort. He turned on the TV, flipping through channels aimlessly. The familiar drone of morning talk shows and sitcom reruns provided a soothing background noise.

As he sat there, his mind began to wander. Flashes of the previous night came back to him in vivid detail—the laughter, the music, the way the girl's eyes sparkled under the bar lights. He remembered their conversation, how they had connected instantly. The mystery of never knowing her name, but the memory of their chemistry was fresh.

He recalled the way she had danced, moving with a grace that mesmerized him. Their conversations had flowed effortlessly, their bodies naturally drawn to each other. The night had ended in a whirlwind of passion, He treated her the way he imagined treating Jessica for the last eight years.

He made her his nasty little slut, her crawling on her knees begging him to choke her with his manhood. Slapping her across the face with it and spitting in her mouth. The night ended with her legs pretzeled behind her head, his cum all over her from forehead to bellybutton.

Chaz closed his eyes, allowing the memories to wash over him. But soon, his thoughts shifted to the time he had spent in prison. Eight years felt like a lifetime. The rigid routines, the constant vigilance, the longing for freedom—all of it had shaped him in ways he was still coming to terms with.

He thought about the friends he had made inside, the alliances that had kept him safe. Chaz had learned to navigate the complex social dynamics of prison life, using his charm and street smarts to avoid trouble. But the isolation had taken its toll, leaving him with a deep sense of loneliness and a yearning for connection.

Chaz made his decision: he was going to stay with Edwin and Jessica. With the determination forged from eight years of solitude, he resolved to move forward with a plan he'd meticulously crafted—a plan to manipulate and deceive those who had once dismissed him. As he paced around Raphael's apartment, he talked to himself, recounting every person in his immediate life who had wronged him.

"Cassie," he muttered, his voice low and bitter. "She never told me how she felt back then. If I'd known the truth, things might have turned out differently. Her silence cost me more than she'll ever know."

He thought back to Edwin, his supposed family. "Edwin treated me like I wasn't part of his family. Even now, he acts as if I'm lower than dirt, as if I don't deserve to be related to him. His contempt has always been obvious."

Jessica's image flickered in his mind. "Jessica never did anything directly to me, but she never stood up for me either. When Edwin and others bullied me, she would sometimes laugh. Her complicity hurt just as much as their actions."

The memories of Chaz's past, the slights, and humiliations, fueled his resolve. Chaz had spent years in prison, honing his mind and body, preparing for the day he would reclaim control over his life. He had envisioned this moment countless times, plotting how he would turn the tables on those who had underestimated him.

Moving in with Edwin and Jessica was the first step. He needed to get close, to gain their trust, and then dismantle their lives from the inside out. The idea of living under the same roof as Edwin, of pretending to accept his condescending kindness, made Chaz's blood boil. But he knew he had to play the long game. His patience and self-control would be his greatest weapons.

Chaz texted Raphael, letting him know that he had decided to move in with his brother Edwin and Jessica. He explained that while he would have liked to stay with Raphael, the apartment was too small for both of them. Raphael responded quickly, assuring Chaz that he understood and would be home in a few hours. He offered to accompany Chaz to Edwin and Jessica's place, providing some much-needed moral support.

The ride to Edwin and Jessica's house felt like an eternity. Chaz stared out the window, his mind racing with thoughts of the past and the uncertain future. He replayed his plan in his head, determined to manipulate and deceive those who had once dismissed him. As the car approached the house, he took a deep breath, summoning the charm and humility he would need to pull this off.

Raphael, sensing Chaz's anxiety, placed a reassuring hand on his shoulder. "You got this, brother. This is just the first step to a better future with your family. Keep taking those good steps forward."

Chaz nodded, grateful for Raphael's unyielding support. As they walked up to the front door, he could feel his heart pounding in his chest. When Jessica opened the door, her face lit up with a welcoming smile. "Chaz! It's so good to see you. Come in, come in."

Edwin was in the living room, and his greeting was polite but distant. "Welcome, Chaz. We're glad you decided to stay with us. Make yourself at home."

"Thank you, Edwin. Jessica," Chaz said, his voice warm and sincere. "I really appreciate you both giving me a place to stay. It means a lot."

Raphael stayed for a while, chatting with Edwin and Jessica, helping ease the initial awkwardness. Chaz felt a mix of relief and determination. He knew he had to play his role perfectly.

Once Raphael left, Chaz began to settle into his new environment. The guest room was modest but comfortable, a stark contrast to the stark, cold cells he had endured for the past eight years. He unpacked his few belongings with meticulous care, each item a small step toward reclaiming his life.

Over the next few month, Chaz played the part of the grateful family member to perfection. He helped around the house, engaged in polite conversation, and expressed genuine gratitude for their hospitality. He even shared a few carefully curated stories from prison, designed to elicit sympathy without revealing too much. Jessica seemed genuinely touched, while Edwin remained cautiously distant, but Chaz could see the cracks in his facade.

One evening, as they sat down for dinner, the conversation turned to family and the future. Chaz seized the opportunity. "I've been thinking a lot about what comes next," he said, his tone thoughtful. "I want to make amends for the past and build a better future for all of us."

Jessica smiled warmly. "That's wonderful, Chaz. We're here to support you every step of the way."

Edwin nodded, though his eyes remained wary. "Yes, we are."

Chaz continued to weave his narrative, subtly planting seeds of doubt and division. He spoke of the importance of family, the need for unity, and the dangers of mistrust. He played on their emotions, exploiting their weaknesses, and slowly but surely, he began to see the effects of his manipulation.

Cassie, meanwhile, remained a distant figure in his mind. He knew he would have to deal with her eventually, to confront the unresolved feelings between them. But for now, his focus was on Edwin and Jessica, on tearing down the walls they had built around their perfect life.

As the weeks went by, Chaz's presence in the house became a constant reminder of the past they had tried to forget. Tensions simmered beneath the surface, small disagreements turned into heated arguments, and the veneer of their harmonious life began to crack. Chaz watched with satisfaction as the seeds he had planted started to bear fruit.

One night, after a particularly tense dinner, Chaz retreated to his room, feeling a sense of triumph. He could hear Edwin and Jessica arguing softly in the living room, their voices a mix of frustration and confusion. He knew it was only a matter of time before their relationship began to unravel completely.

"Why aren't you around anymore, Edwin?" Jessica's voice was strained with irritation.

Edwin sighed heavily. "I didn't want Chaz here in the first place. You insisted, so you deal with him. Maybe if you'd listened to me, things would be different."

"Are you seriously blaming me for this? He's your brother, Edwin. He needed help."

"Help, yes. Moving in, no. You wanted this, Jessica. You wanted to play the savior."

Their words cut through the walls, each one a knife in the fragile fabric of their relationship. Chaz could almost see the tension snapping, the bond between them unraveling.

As he lay in bed, Chaz allowed himself a rare moment of reflection. The path he had chosen was dark and twisted, but it was the only way he knew to reclaim his power. He had been a victim for too long, and now it was his turn to be in control. The people who had wronged him would pay for their actions, and he would emerge from the shadows stronger than ever.

Sleep came slowly, but when it did, it was filled with dreams of a future where he was no longer bound by the chains of his past. Chaz knew that the road ahead would be challenging, but he was ready to face whatever came his way. With each passing day, his resolve grew stronger, his plan more concrete. The game had begun, and he was determined to win.

Eager to rebuild his life on his own terms, Chaz made calls, set up appointments, and even found a potential job that intrigued him. Each small step he took was a foundation for a new beginning. He meticulously planned his days, ensuring that every action contributed to his long-term goals. The job he found was more than just a way to make ends meet; it represented an opportunity to redefine himself and carve out a future distinct from his troubled past.

Chaz's efforts were not just about securing employment; they were about reclaiming his sense of purpose and control. He knew that the road ahead would be challenging, but he was determined to face it head-on. The satisfaction he derived from his progress was palpable, and it fueled his resolve to continue pushing forward.

As Chaz focused on his personal growth, the dynamics within the house continued to shift. The tension between him and the others became more pronounced, with each conflict revealing deeper resentments and unanswered issues. The once-stable environment was now fraught with unease, as everyone grappled with the changes Chaz's return had triggered.

Despite the growing discord, Chaz remained steadfast in his pursuit of a better life. He saw the arguments and conflicts as necessary steps in the process of moving forward. Each confrontation was an opportunity to address the past and clear the way for a future unburdened by old grievances.

As he lay on the couch, Chaz reflected on the day. He realized that while the road ahead was uncertain, he was no longer alone. He had friends, family, and a newfound sense of purpose guiding him forward. The night's memories faded into the background, replaced by the anticipation of what tomorrow might bring.

Chaz drifted off to sleep with a smile on his face, ready to face whatever challenges and opportunities came his way. The past was behind him, and a new future awaited. Despite the growing discord between Edwin and Jessica, Chaz found himself growing closer to Jessica. Her kindness and empathy contrasted sharply with Edwin's cold distance. She began confiding in Chaz, sharing her frustrations and worries, and Chaz listened, offering comfort, and understanding.

Raphael checked in regularly, becoming a frequent visitor, his presence a balm to Chaz's troubled mind. They spent hours talking about the future, about Chaz's plans and aspirations. With offering support and encouragement their bond grew stronger, proof to the loyalty and friendship that had sustained Chaz through his darkest times.

CHAPTER 6

Chaz opened the door and froze at the sight before him. Standing there was Raphael, behind him was Cassie, the woman who had recently confessed her love for him in a heartfelt letter while he was in prison. The shock of seeing her with Raphael was like a punch to the gut, leaving Chaz reeling and unsure of how to react. His mind raced with conflicting thoughts and emotions. He had believed Cassie loved him, yet here she was, seemingly involved with Raphael.

"Hey bro," Raphael greeted with his usual warmth, oblivious to Chaz's internal commotion. "Not sure if you remember Cassie from our high school days."

Chaz forced a smile, struggling to mask his confusion and frustration. "Oh, hey Cassie. Long time no see," he replied, his voice betraying none of the storm raging inside him. "How long has it been? Eight years, right? Before I went away."

Cassie nodded, her expression neutral. "That sounds about right. It's good to see you doing better."

Raphael looked around and then back at Chaz. "Can we come in?"

Hesitating for a moment, Chaz finally stepped aside. "Sure, come in."

They moved to the living room, an awkward silence settling over them as they took their seats. Chaz's mind was still in overdrive, trying to make sense of the situation. He wanted to protect Raphael from any hurt but also felt a burning desire to confront Cassie about her apparent duplicity.

Breaking the silence, Chaz asked, "How do you two know each other?"

Raphael leaned back, stretching his arms across the back of the couch. "When I moved back to the city, I looked up a few people I used to know before I moved away. Cassie was one of them. We started hanging out, and it's just recently that we've become more... but no title yet."

Cassie nodded in agreement. "Yeah, no title yet."

Chaz's mind buzzed with questions. Did she know Raphael and I were in contact? Did she realize the implications of her actions? If she knew and still went ahead, then maybe she deserved whatever consequences came her way. But if she didn't know, it made things complicated in a different way.

Cassie interrupted his thoughts. "What happened, Chaz? The last thing I remember was you being there one day and gone the next. There were a lot of rumors, but nothing concrete. I asked your brother, but he just acted like you didn't exist anymore."

Chaz sighed, the weight of his past pressing down on him. "Well, you know how I was always by myself for the most part. I used to disappear for maybe a month or less, usually ending up in juvie for different reasons. Fights, getting blamed for starting them when I was the one getting bullied. My brother never wanted me around, so he never stood up for me. There were also possession charges, small amounts of weed at first. Then I started hanging with the wrong people, selling more. I was a loner, very smart but socially awkward. After everything I went through in high school, I became a man who could never get himself together. In and out of juvie until I was sixteen and caught a few drug and gun charges that put me away for eight years. Everyone abandoned. My own family treated me like I didn't matter, wanting nothing to do with me."

As Chaz spoke, he watched Cassie's reaction, looking for any sign of guilt or realization. She listened intently, her eyes showing a mix of empathy and regret. Raphael remained silent, absorbing the gravity of Chaz's story.

The room fell into silence once more, the friction thick enough to cut with a knife. Chaz's mind continued to race. He needed to figure out his next move, how to handle this unexpected twist in his plans. The last thing he wanted was to hurt Raphael, the one person who had never wronged him. But seeing Cassie with him stirred a urge for retribution, a feeling he struggled to suppress.

Cassie broke the silence, her voice soft and filled with regret. "Chaz, I had no idea you were going through all those things. If I had known, I... I don't know what I would have done differently, but we can't change the past. We can only move forward."

Chaz took a deep breath, trying to calm the chaos within. He looked at Raphael, then back at Cassie. "I need some time to process all this. It's opened so many wounds that I thought I worked through years ago."

Raphael nodded, understanding in his eyes. "Of course, bro. We didn't mean to open old wounds. We can give you some space."

Cassie stood up, her expression a mixture of concern and sadness. "I'm really sorry, Chaz. I hope we can talk more when you're ready."

Chaz sighed, feeling the weight of the past pressing down on him. "It's fine. I just didn't think I would have to relive everything I went through so soon. No need to rush out unless you have plans and need to leave."

Raphael glanced at Cassie and then back at Chaz. "We don't have any plans. We're here for you."

As Raphael excused himself to use the bathroom, Chaz seized the moment to confront Cassie. "How could you do this?" he hissed, his voice low but intense. "You wrote me a letter saying you loved me, and now you're with my best friend?"

Cassie looked down, guilt etched on her face. "It wasn't planned, Chaz. After I wrote the letter, things just happened. It wasn't serious at first, but it turned into something right before you came home."

Chaz's anger flared, but he forced himself to stay calm as he heard Raphael returning. He quickly changed his demeanor, masking the intense conversation. Raphael re-entered the room, oblivious to the unease that had just filled the air.

"So," Raphael said, sitting back down, "we need to get together outside of the house, the three of us. Maybe we can even find you a date, Chaz."

Chaz forced a smile, though his mind was still reeling. "Yeah, that sounds good," he replied, his voice steady.

They continued talking, the conversation flowing more easily now, but Chaz couldn't shake the lingering hurt and confusion. As they chatted about old times and future plans, he kept stealing glances at Cassie, wondering how things had gotten even more confusing.

Over the next few days, Chaz tried to focus on getting his life back on track. He was eager to rebuild, but the situation with Cassie and Raphael weighed heavily on his mind. Cassie, a woman he'd known for years and who had confessed her feelings for him, had started seeing Raphael, his closest friend. The emotional turmoil was a constant distraction.

One evening, as Chaz sat on his Queen size bed his phone buzzed. He picked it up and saw a text from Raphael: "Hey man, BBQ at my place this weekend. You in?"

Chaz hesitated, his fingers hovering over the screen. He hadn't seen Raphael since discovering the relationship with Cassie, and he wasn't sure he was ready for this. But he knew avoiding the situation wouldn't help. Taking a deep breath, he replied, "Sure, I'll be there."

Saturday arrived, and Chaz found himself standing outside Raphael's house, nerves gnawing at him. He could hear laughter and smell the aroma of grilled meat wafting through the air. Taking a deep breath, he knocked on the door.

Raphael answered, his face breaking into a warm smile. "Hey, man! Glad you could make it," he said, pulling Chaz into a hug.

"Wouldn't miss it," Chaz replied, returning the hug with a bit of hesitation.

As Chaz stepped into the backyard, he saw a small gathering of people, some familiar faces, and others he didn't recognize. Cassie was there too, and she gave him a tentative smile. He nodded in acknowledgment, feeling a swirl of emotions.

Raphael handed Chaz a beer and guided him to a bench near a pond. "Let's catch up," he said, trying to break the ice.

They joined the others by the grill, the smell of cooking meat mingling with the sounds of laughter and conversation. Chaz tried to relax, reminding himself that this was a chance to move forward.

At one point, Raphael pulled Chaz aside. "I wanted to talk to you about something," he said, his tone serious.

Chaz braced himself. "What's up?"

"Remember the day I found out about you and Cassie?" Raphael began. "What do you think about her? I also invited Jenna over today. I thought you two might hit it off."

Before Chaz could respond, a voice interrupted. "Hi, I'm Jenna," a woman said, extending her hand.

"Chaz," he replied, shaking her hand. "Nice to meet you."

They started talking, and Chaz found himself opening up to her in a way he hadn't with anyone in a long time. Jenna was easy to talk to, and her genuine interest in his story was a welcome change. He told her about his time in prison, his struggles to adjust to life outside, and a little about the tricky situation with Cassie and Raphael.

Jenna listened attentively, offering insights and encouragement. "It sounds like you've been through a lot, but it also sounds like you're trying to move forward. That's what matters."

Chaz nodded, feeling a sense of relief. "Yeah, I guess so. It's just hard sometimes, you know?"

"I do," Jenna said, her eyes reflecting understanding. "But you're not alone. There seems to be people who care about you, and new people you'll meet who will care too."

They spent some time talking, laughing, and getting to know each other. For the first time in a long time, Chaz felt a real glimmer of hope. As the night came to an end, they exchanged numbers, and Jenna gave him a reassuring smile. "Call me if you ever need to talk, okay?"

Chaz nodded. "I will. Thanks, Jenna."

Meanwhile, Raphael remembered that Cassie had mentioned inviting a few friends over as well. As the evening progressed, he saw Cassie walking over with a stunning woman he recognized from a night out with Chaz. His heart skipped a beat as they approached.

"Raphael, I'd like you to meet my best friend, Vanessa," Cassie said, a hint of pride in her voice.

Vanessa smiled warmly. "Nice to meet you, Raphael. Cassie has told me so much about you."

Raphael forced a smile, trying to hide his surprise. "Nice to meet you as well. Cassie always speaks highly of you."

As small talk ensued, Raphael couldn't help but feel a strange mix of emotions. He remembered the night he'd met Vanessa, "Beautiful Lounge Owner," and the undeniable attraction he'd felt. But now, here she was, introduced to him as Cassie's best friend.

Cassie excused herself, leaving Raphael and Vanessa alone. "So, how do you know Cassie?" Raphael asked, trying to steer the conversation to safer grounds.

"We've been friends since grade school," Vanessa replied. "She's been a rock for me through everything."

"That's great. Cassie is an amazing person," Raphael said, feeling a pang of guilt for the situation.

Finally, Vanessa broke the nice girl routine, her voice quiet but intense. "Raphael, why didn't you say anything about your relationship with Cassie?"

Raphael looked up from stacking chairs, his expression serious. "Vanessa, it's not what you think. Cassie and I aren't in a relationship."

Vanessa crossed her arms, her eyes searching his face. "I know the whole situation, Raphael. Cassie is my best friend. If I knew it was you that she was involved with, I wouldn't have kept communicating. It's... touch-and-go."

Raphael sighed, running a hand through his beard. "It is problematic. Cassie and I... It started as something casual, a distraction maybe, but it's not a relationship. We both know that. We've talked about it."

Vanessa's expression softened, but confusion and frustration still lingered. "But why didn't you tell me? When we first met, why didn't you mention Cassie?"

"Because I didn't think it would matter," Raphael admitted. "When we first met, I didn't know how things would evolve. I didn't expect to feel this way about you."

Vanessa looked away, her thoughts racing. "Cassie told me about her feelings for Chaz. She's been so conflicted. And now, finding out about you... it's a lot to process. I don't want to hurt her, but I also can't ignore what I'm starting to feel."

Raphael stepped closer, his voice low and earnest. "Vanessa, what do you mean feelings for Chaz? Cassie never said anything about feelings for him to me."

Vanessa said to Raphael, "I wasn't supposed to say anything about Cassie having feelings for Chaz."

Raphael's eyes widened, caught off guard by Vanessa's slip. A flood of questions surged through his mind. Did Chaz know Cassie had feelings for him? How long have they been in contact with each other? And why hadn't either of them mentioned it to him? Is this why Chaz had been acting strange since he saw me with Cassie?

Unsure of what to think, Raphael watched from a distance for the rest of the night. He kept an eye on

Cassie, observing her every move, trying to piece together the puzzle forming in his mind.

The evening wore on, Chaz found himself gravitating back to Jenna. Her presence was soothing to his troubled mind. They talked about their favorite books, movies, and life experiences, and Chaz realized how much he had missed simple, genuine conversations.

Raphael watched from a distance, feeling a sense of relief. Seeing that Chaz was occupied with Jenna, hoping that she could keep his attention and keep him away from Cassie. But in the back his mind the feelings for Vanessa were growing more complicated by the minute.

The barbecue eventually wound down, and guests began to leave. Chaz walked over to Raphael, feeling a sense of closure. "Thanks for inviting me, man. I needed this," he said.

"Anytime, Chaz. I'm glad you came," Raphael replied, clapping him on the back.

Chaz then approached Jenna, who was gathering her things. "Can I walk you to your car?" he asked.

"Sure," she said, smiling.

Before heading to her car, Chaz excused himself. He walked over to Cassie, thanked her for the invite, and leaned into whisper in her ear, "We need to get together soon. We have a lot to figure out."

Out of the corner of his eye, Raphael noticed the interaction but chose to keep this little secret to himself. He decided to wait until he could figure out how to handle Cassie's lies and determine if his best friend knew about her feelings for Chaz.

They walked down the block to her car, and Jenna said, "I'm really glad we met."

"Me too," Chaz replied. "We should get together sometime, maybe a double date."

"Sure, let's plan something," Jenna agreed. "Have a good night, Chaz."

"You too. Get home safe," Chaz responded.

Back at the apartment, Raphael, Cassie, and Vanessa were cleaning up the last of the barbecue remnants. When Cassie went inside, Raphael seized the opportunity to talk to Vanessa.

"You know," Raphael said, breaking the silence, "I'm glad we got to meet like this. I found out some things I needed to know."

"Me too," Vanessa admitted. "It's been... enlightening."

Raphael laughed softly, but there was an edge to it. "Life has a funny way of bringing people together, doesn't it?"

"Yeah, it does," Vanessa agreed, then hesitated. "Please don't say anything to Cassie about what I told you."

Raphael's eyes glinted as he leaned in closer. "I won't, as long as you don't stop our communication."

"That's not right," Vanessa said, her voice trembling.

"You want something, and I want something," Raphael replied, his tone firm.

Before Vanessa could respond, Cassie rejoined them, ready to finish so she and Vanessa could head home.

As Cassie and Vanessa left, Raphael watched them go, his mind racing with plans and calculations. He knew he had to confront Cassie about her lies, about Chaz, and about her feelings. But more than that, he couldn't shake the growing attraction he felt towards Vanessa.

Turning back to the empty apartment, Raphael began to strategize. He would keep Vanessa close, using manipulation if necessary to ensure she didn't pull away. He needed to uncover whether Chaz had known about Cassie's feelings all along or if Cassie had deceived everyone.

Deep down, Raphael knew he was playing a dangerous game, but he was determined to navigate it to his advantage. As he paced the room, plotting his next move, the weight of his decision settled heavily on his shoulders. The cage of relationships and emotions he found himself in were far from simple, and the path ahead was fraught with uncertainty.

But Raphael was not one to shy away from complexity. With a steely resolve, he vowed to unravel the truth, no matter the cost.

CHAPTER 7

One morning, Chaz woke up to a text from Raphael, he sent better job leads and contact information for a support group that might help. Chaz felt a surge of gratitude for more hope in his otherwise bleak situation.

Before heading out to follow up on these leads, Chaz ran into Jessica in the kitchen. Her presence had always been a source of comfort amidst the chaos. "Morning, Jessica. How are you doing?" he asked, trying to keep the conversation light.

Jessica looked up from her coffee, her eyes softening at the sight of him. "Morning, Chaz. I'm okay. I know things have been rough, but once I get a better job I can work my way into my own place," he added, hoping to ease her burden.

"Chaz, there's no rush for you to leave," Jessica said, her voice gentle. "Your brother should just get used to you being around for a little bit. It's a pleasure to have you here."

The animosity between Edwin and Chaz continued to grow. Edwin couldn't shake the feeling that his brother's presence was a ticking time bomb, waiting to explode. He often found himself arguing with Jessica about it, unable to understand why she was so insistent on helping Chaz.

Jessica, on the other hand, saw a side of Chaz that Edwin refused to acknowledge. She saw a man trying to rebuild his life, to find a place where he belonged. Her heart ached for him, and she couldn't stand the thought of turning him away.

Chaz and Jessica began to spend more time together. Their conversations, initially casual and brief, grew longer and more personal. They talked about their dreams, their fears, and the burdens they carried. Jessica found herself opening up to Chaz in ways she never had with Edwin.

Edwin started to notice the growing distance between him and Jessica. She seemed distracted, often lost in thought. And it didn't escape his notice that when Jessica wasn't around, neither was Chaz. The realization gnawed at him, fueling his suspicions and jealousy.

One evening, after a particularly heated argument with Edwin, Jessica retreated to the backyard. She found Chaz there, staring up at the stars. "Rough night?" he asked, his voice soothing to her frayed nerves.

"You could say that." she sighed, sitting down next to him. "Edwin and I... we just can't seem to agree on anything these days."

Chaz turned to her, his eyes filled with genuine concern. "I'm sorry, Jessica. I never wanted to come between you two."

"You haven't," she said quickly, reaching out to touch his arm. "It's just... complicated."

They sat in silence for a while, the night enveloping them in its quiet embrace. Jessica felt a strange sense of peace with Chaz, a feeling she hadn't experienced in a long time.

Chaz and Jessica found solace in each other's company, an escape from the awkward tension that plagued the house. One afternoon, while Edwin was at work, Jessica and Chaz found themselves alone again.

They were in the kitchen, preparing lunch. The radio played softly in the background, filling the room with a sense of normalcy. Jessica laughed at something Chaz said, the sound light and carefree. For a moment, everything felt perfect.

Chaz watched her, a smile tugging at his lips. "You know, Jessica, you have the most beautiful laugh."

She blushed, looking down at the cutting board in front of her. "Thank you, Chaz. You always know how to make me smile."

Their eyes met, and in that instant, something shifted. The air between them crackled with an unspoken longing. Chaz took a step closer, his heart pounding in his chest. "Jessica..."

Before he could finish, she closed the distance between them, pressing her lips to his. The kiss was soft and tentative at first, a gentle exploration of emotions they could no longer deny. But it quickly deepened, fueled by months of suppressed longing.

When they finally pulled apart, both were breathless, their hearts racing. Jessica's eyes were wide with a mixture of fear and excitement. "Chaz, we can't..."

"I know," he whispered, his voice hoarse. "But I can't stop thinking about you."

"Me neither," she admitted, her voice barely audible.

From that moment on, Chaz and Jessica's affair became an intoxicating secret they couldn't resist. They stole moments whenever they could, their passion burning brighter with each stolen kiss and whispered confession.

They were careful, always mindful of Edwin's presence. But the guilt weighed heavily on Jessica. She loved Edwin, but her feelings for Chaz were undeniable, a force she couldn't control.

Edwin, oblivious to the affair, continued to grow more distant. He could sense something was off, but he couldn't put his finger on it. The discomfort in the house was reaching a breaking point, and he was desperate to find a solution.

As Chaz and Jessica's connection deepened, their physical attraction became impossible to ignore. It began with lingering touches and heated glances that spoke volumes. Every time their fingers brushed, a spark ignited between them, sending their hearts racing. Their craving was a dangerous, intoxicating secret that added a thrilling edge to their everyday interactions.

One particularly tense evening, Edwin had gone to bed early after another argument with Jessica about Chaz. As the house settled into silence, Jessica found herself restless, unable to sleep. She slipped out of bed and found Chaz in the living room, the dim light from the TV casting shadows across his face.

"Can't sleep either?" he asked softly, looking up at her.

She shook her head, her heart pounding. "No, I can't."

Without another word, Chaz stood and crossed the room, his eyes locked onto hers. He reached out, brushing a strand of hair from her face. The touch was electric, sending shivers down her spine.

"Jessica," he whispered, his voice thick with emotion.

"Chaz, we can't..." she started, but her protest was weak, her resolve crumbling under the intensity of his gaze.

"I know," he said, leaning in closer. "But I can't fight this anymore."

Before she could respond, his lips were on hers, the kiss igniting a fire that had been smoldering for months. It was a kiss born of desperation and longing, a release of all the pent-up emotions they had been harboring. Jessica melted into his arms, her body responding to his touch with an urgency that matched his own.

That night marked the beginning of their physical relationship. They moved to the couch, their kisses growing more heated and frantic. Chaz's hands roamed over her body, exploring every curve and contour, while Jessica's fingers tangled in his hair, pulling him closer.

They undressed each other with a mix of eagerness and tenderness, the barriers between them falling away. Chaz's touch was both gentle and possessive, his hands tracing patterns on her skin that made her gasp. Jessica responded with equal fervor, her body arching into his as they moved together.

The nature of Chaz and Jessica's affair only intensified their passion for one another. Their secret trysts were a game of cat and mouse, adding a dangerous and exhilarating edge to their encounters. Every stolen moment was filled with an urgent, frantic passion that made their lovemaking even more electrifying.

They communicated through silent signals, a system they had perfected over time. A door left slightly ajar, or a light left on was Chaz's invitation to Jessica. She would wait until the house was shrouded in darkness, slipping into his room with the stealth of a shadow.

Their first encounter in Jessica's room was a blur of unifed limbs and hushed whispers. Chaz's hands roamed over her body with a hunger that matched her own, their kisses deep and consuming. The urgency of their need for each other drove them to the brink, their bodies coming together in a whirlwind of passion.

Every subsequent encounter was a race against time, their hunger a force of nature that couldn't be contained. They found hidden corners of the house to satisfy their lust, from the laundry room to the basement, each location adding a new layer of excitement to their affair.

One memorable night, they found themselves in the kitchen, the soft hum of the refrigerator the only sound in the otherwise silent house. Chaz lifted Jessica onto the counter, his lips trailing hot kisses down her neck as she wrapped her legs around his waist. The cool surface of the counter contrasted with the heat of their bodies, making the experience even more intense.

They made love with intenseness that bordered on obsession, exploring each other's bodies with a thoroughness that left them both breathless. Chaz's touch was both gentle and demanding, his fingers tracing every curve and dip of Jessica's form. She responded with equal commitment, her nails digging into his back as they moved together in perfect harmony, his hands pulling her hair while thrusting into her.

He lays her back as he continues to thrust his manhood deeper and deeper, his hands around her neck choking her with pleasure. He lifts her up, her arms wrapped around his neck, placing her feet onto the ground. He forcefully turns her around and bends her over.

She knew who was in control. Guiding him into her waterfall one hand pulling her hair so he can watch her eye rolling into the back of her head and the other hand spanking her juicy plump ass.

As they finished it was like fireworks from the Fourth of July erupted inside her. The loud scream she let off could be heard down the street as she said Chaz's name.

After their passionate encounters, they would lie together in the afterglow, their bodies intertwined. These quiet moments were just as important as the physical act itself, allowing them to connect on a deeper level. They talked about their hopes and fears, their dreams, and regrets, finding solace in each other's arms.

Chaz found a sense of belonging with Jessica that he had never felt before. She understood him in ways that Edwin never could, offering him the support and compassion he desperately needed. Jessica, in turn, felt seen and appreciated in a way that Edwin had never made her feel. Their affair became a lifeline, a secret sanctuary where they could be their true selves.

The height of their affair came on a stormy afternoon when Edwin was away on a business trip. The rain poured down in sheets, creating a cocoon of privacy that heightened their senses. The house felt like their own private world, free from the prying eyes of judgment.

They made love with wildly, their bodies entwined as the storm raged outside. The sound of the rain against the windows and the distant rumble of thunder added to the passion of the moment. It was as if the world outside had ceased to exist, leaving only the two of them and their insatiable thirst for each other.

Despite the depth of their physical and emotional connection, both Chaz and Jessica knew their affair couldn't last forever. The secrecy, the guilt, and the constant fear of discovery were taking their toll. They began to talk about the future, about what would happen when the truth inevitably came out.

Jessica was torn. She loved Edwin and didn't want to hurt him, but her feelings for Chaz were undeniable. She couldn't imagine a future without him.

As their affair escalated, the deception grew more intricate. Chaz reveled in the satisfaction of exacting his revenge on Edwin who always dismissed him and acted like he didn't exist. Jessica, fueled by a mixture of lust and recklessness, willingly played her part in this dangerous game.

CHAPTER 8

Raphael's first step was to deepen his connection with Vanessa. He knew she was torn between her loyalty to Cassie and the developing feelings she harbored for him. He began texting her more frequently, their conversations growing increasingly intimate. He played on her vulnerabilities, listening to her concerns about her businesses, offering advice, and providing a comforting ear.

"Hey Vanessa, how's your day going?" Raphael texted one afternoon, knowing she was likely in the miffle of her busy schedule.

"Hey Raphael. It's been hectic, as usual. Trying to juggle a million things at once," she replied almost immediately, a sign that she was waiting for an outlet to release her stress.

"I can imagine. Your dedication is impressive though. How's the lounge doing?" He wanted to make her feel seen and appreciated.

"Thanks, Raphael. The lounge is doing well, but there's always something that needs my attention. Sometimes it feels like there's no end to it," Vanessa confessed, the weight of her responsibilities evident in her words.

"I get that. Running a business is no small feat. Remember, it's okay to take a break sometimes. You deserve it," Raphael advised, his tone gentle yet firm.

"I know, I know. It's just hard to step away when everything feels so dependent on me," Vanessa admitted.

"You're doing an amazing job. But don't forget to take care of yourself too. If you ever need to talk or vent, I'm here," Raphael offered, hoping to be her anchor in the storm.

"I appreciate that. It means a lot coming from you. Sometimes it feels like you're the only one who really understands what I'm going through," Vanessa responded, her words a mix of gratitude and vulnerability.

"I'm glad I can be that person for you. You've been through so much, and it's important to have someone who can support you," Raphael assured her, sensing the bond between them growing stronger.

"Thank you, Raphael. Your support really helps. How about you? How have you been?" Vanessa asked, turning the conversation towards him.

"I've been good. Just thinking a lot about us and everything that's been happening. I want to make sure you're okay with everything," he replied, steering the conversation towards their complex relationship.

"It's confusing, you know? With Cassie and everything. I don't want to hurt her," Vanessa confessed, the guilt weighing heavily on her.

"I understand. It's a tricky situation. But I care about you, Vanessa. And I want to be there for you in any way I can," Raphael said earnestly, hoping to ease her burden.

"I care about you too, Raphael. It's just hard to navigate these feelings when there's so much at stake," Vanessa admitted, her emotions a tangled mess.

"We'll figure it out together. Just take it one step at a time. And remember, I'm here for you, no matter what," Raphael promised, determined to be her source of strength and comfort.

Raphael's constant presence became a cornerstone for Vanessa. She found herself looking forward to their conversations, feeling lighter each time they talked. His understanding and support were unlike anything she had experienced before. It was intoxicating, this mix of friendship and accelerating affection.

Vanessa's loyalty to Cassie made every step with Raphael feel like walking on a tightrope. She knew Cassie was deeply invested in figuring out her situation with Chaz, but the emotional distance created a void that Raphael seemed to fill effortlessly.

One evening, after a particularly grueling day, Vanessa received another text from Raphael. "How was today? Did you manage to find a moment to breathe?"

Vanessa smiled, feeling a warmth spread through her. "Barely, but your texts help. It feels like you're right here with me."

Raphael's response was almost immediate. "I'm always with you in spirit, Vanessa. Remember that. We'll get through this together."

Vanessa found herself more entangled in Raphael's comforting words and genuine care. The path ahead was fraught with challenges, but with Raphael by her side, she felt a glimmer of hope that maybe, just maybe, they could navigate this complex journey together.

Vanessa, despite her reservations, found herself drawn to Raphael. He was charismatic and attentive in a way she hadn't experienced before. The guilt gnawed at her, but she couldn't deny the connection they shared. She rationalized that as long as nothing physical happened, she wasn't truly betraying Cassie.

Meanwhile, Raphael kept a close eye on Cassie. He began subtly questioning her about Chaz, trying to gauge her true feelings. Cassie, preoccupied with her own internal struggle, didn't suspect Raphael's ulterior motives. She was grappling with her emotions, torn between her affection for Raphael and the unresolved feelings she had for Chaz.

Raphael's plan was working. He was slowly driving a wedge between Cassie and Vanessa while keeping both women within his grasp. He knew it was only a matter of time before reaching the breaking point.

One evening, Raphael invited Vanessa to his apartment under the pretense of discussing a potential business collaboration. Vanessa hesitated but eventually agreed. When she arrived, she was nervous but intrigued. Raphael greeted her warmly, offering her a glass of wine.

They sat on the couch, talking about their lives and ambitions. The conversation flowed effortlessly, the atmosphere charged. As the evening wore on, Raphael leaned in closer, his hand brushing against hers.

"Vanessa, you know there's something between us," he murmured, his voice low and enticing.

Vanessa's breath hitched. She knew this was the moment she had feared and anticipated. "Raphael, this isn't right," she said, her voice trembling.

Raphael cupped her face in his hands, his eyes locking onto hers. "Right and wrong are just constructs. What we feel is real. You can't deny it."

Before she could respond, he kissed her. The kiss was electric, igniting a fire within her. Vanessa's resolve crumbled as she gave in to the passion that had been building between them.

That night, their relationship crossed the line from emotional to physical. Vanessa was overwhelmed with a mix of envy and guilt, knowing she had betrayed her best friend but unable to resist the pull of her feelings for Raphael.

The adventures between Raphael and Vanessa continued in secret. They met whenever they could, their encounters filled with a mix of passion and excitement. Vanessa was constantly on edge, fearing Cassie would find out, but she couldn't bring herself to end things with Raphael.

Raphael, reveled in the control he had over both women. He continued his relationship with Cassie, who remained oblivious to the affair. He used his time with her to gather more information about Chaz, hoping to use it to his advantage.

One evening, while lying in bed with Vanessa, Raphael broached the subject of Cassie. "Do you think she still has feelings for Chaz?" he asked casually.

Vanessa tensed. "I don't know. She never talks about it with me."

Raphael's eyes narrowed. He knew Vanessa was hiding something, but he decided not to press the issue. He had other ways of uncovering the truth.

In the upcoming weeks, the distance between Cassie and Vanessa grew. Cassie sensed that something was off but couldn't put her finger on it. She confided in Raphael, seeking reassurance and support.

"I feel like Vanessa is keeping something from me," Cassie said one evening, her brow furrowed in concern.

Raphael's heart raced, but he maintained a calm facade. "Maybe she's just stressed with work. You know how much pressure she's under."

Cassie nodded, but the doubt lingered. She couldn't shake the feeling that something was wrong.

Days passed, Raphael decided to surprise Vanessa at the lounge while it was closed. He snuck up behind her, gently placing his hands over her eyes. "Guess who," he whispered playfully.

Vanessa turned around, recognizing his voice instantly. Without hesitation, she pulled him into an intense kiss. After a moment, she pulled back, breathless. "Grab a drink," she said, her eyes sparkling with mischief. "I'll be right back."

She returned moments later, carrying a drink she had made for herself to join him. "Rough day?" he asked, his voice low and soothing as he took off his jacket.

"You have no idea," she sighed, running a hand through her hair. "I just need to unwind."

"Then let me help you," Raphael said, stepping closer.

Vanessa felt her pulse quicken as he closed the distance between them. His hand reached up to gently cup her face, his thumb caressing against her cheek. She leaned into his touch, her eyes closing as she felt the warmth of his palm.

"You're always so strong," he murmured. "It's okay to let go sometimes."

His words were a relief to her soul, and she found herself nodding, her breath buckling slightly. "I know," she whispered, opening her eyes to meet his gaze.

Raphael's eyes were filled with an assertiveness that made her knees weak. He leaned in slowly, giving her time to pull away if she wanted to, but she didn't. Instead, she tilted her head up to meet him halfway, their lips brushing softly at first. The kiss deepened quickly, a flood of pent-up emotion and passion pouring out of both of them.

Vanessa's hands found their way to Raphael's shoulders, gripping him tightly as he pulled her closer. His arms wrapped around her waist, holding her firmly against him. The kiss grew more urgent, their tongues dancing together as they explored this intoxicating connection.

Their lips never parting for long. Raphael's hands roamed her back, finding the zipper of her dress and slowly pulling it down. Vanessa shivered at the sensation, a thrill of anticipation running through her. She shrugged out of the dress, letting it fall to the floor as she reached for Raphael's shirt, unbuttoning it with trembling fingers.

He helped her, shrugging off his shirt and tossing it aside before his hands were on her again, exploring the newly revealed skin. Vanessa felt a fire within her as his hands caressed her, his touch sending sparks of pleasure through her body.

They stumbled their way to one of the couches, falling onto the soft cushions in a tangle of limbs.

Raphael's mouth trailed down her neck, leaving a trail of fiery kisses that made her moan softly. Her hands were busy exploring his body, feeling the hard planes of his chest and the firm muscles of his back.

Raphael's lips found their way to her breasts, kissing and sucking gently, eliciting soft gasps from Vanessa. His hands tangled in her hair, holding her as he lavished attention on her sensitive nipples. The sensation was almost too much, she arched her back, pressing herself closer to him.

He continued his descent, his mouth leaving a scorching path down her stomach until he reached the waistband of her panties. He looked up at her, his eyes dark with desire, silently asking for permission. She nodded, lifting her hips to help him slide the panties off.

Raphael took his time, kissing the inside of her thighs, his breath hot against her skin. Vanessa's anticipation built with every touch, every kiss. When his mouth finally found her core, she cried out, her hands clutching the cushions as pleasure overwhelmed her.

He worked her skillfully, his tongue and lips bringing her to the edge again and again. Vanessa felt like she was on fire, every nerve ending alight with pleasure. When he finally pulled back, she was trembling, her body aching for more.

Raphael climbed back up her body, his eyes never leaving hers. He positioned himself at her entrance, pausing to make sure she was ready. She wrapped her legs around him, pulling him closer, her eyes pleading for him to continue.

He entered her slowly, the sensation making them both gasp. Raphael moved with a deliberate, steady rhythm, each thrust bringing them closer together. Vanessa's hands roamed his back, her nails digging in slightly as the pleasure built.

Their movements became more frantic, their breaths mingling in a symphony of passion. Vanessa felt herself climbing higher, the pleasure becoming almost unbearable. Raphael's pace quickened, his own need evident in his every movement.

When they finally reached the peak, it was like an explosion. Vanessa cried out, her body trembling as waves of pleasure crashed over her. Raphael followed moments later, his body shuddering with the force of his release.

They lay together afterwards, their bodies entwined, the intensity of the moment still lingering in the air. Raphael held her close, his hand gently stroking her hair as they caught their breath.

"That was incredible," Vanessa whispered, her voice filled with awe and satisfaction.

"It was," Raphael agreed, his voice equally soft. "You're incredible."

Vanessa smiled, feeling a sense of peace and contentment she hadn't felt in a long time. She knew there were challenges ahead, but for now, in Raphael's arms, she felt like everything would be okay.

CHAPTER 9

Cassie sat at the window of her small apartment, staring out at the sunset. The soft glow of the setting sunbathed the skyline in hues of orange and pink, creating a peaceful contrast to the storm brewing in her heart. She finally decided to take Vanessa's advice to heart, realizing that she could no longer continue living in the limbo of her own making. It was time to explore her feelings for both Raphael and Chaz without the pressure of immediate decisions. The journey promised twists and turns that neither she nor the men in her life could foresee.

Raphael had entered her life at a time when she felt most vulnerable. He was charming, attentive, and passionate. Their relationship had blossomed slowly, but the passion grew quickly, igniting a flame that seemed to burn brighter with each passing day. When they were together, Cassie felt a deep connection, an intense attraction that made her feel alive. They shared moments of passion that left her breathless, but there was more to their bond than just physical chemistry. Raphael understood her in ways she hadn't anticipated, his words often resonating with unspoken emotions she had buried deep within.

Meanwhile, Chaz had always been a looming presence in her thoughts, even during his time away. Their history was complicated, filled with unspoken words and lingering emotions. When Cassie had written to him, confessing her long-held feelings, she had not expected a reply. But Chaz had responded, and his words had opened a floodgate of memories and emotions. His imminent release from prison brought forth difficult conversations and moments of reflection, forcing Cassie to confront the past and its implications on their future.

Cassie found herself walking a tightrope between two very different relationships. With Raphael, the path was filled with passion and connection, while with Chaz, it was a journey through memories and emotions. She decided to give herself the space to explore both relationships, hoping that clarity would come with time.

Cassie planned a quiet night in with Raphael. They cooked dinner together, laughing and sharing stories over a bottle of wine. As they sat on the couch, the moon and city lights shining bright through the window, Raphael took her hand, his eyes filled with a mix of affection and eagerness.

"Cassie," he said softly, "I know things have been complicated lately, but I want you to know that I'm here for you, no matter what."

She smiled, squeezing his hand. "Thank you, Raphael. That means a lot to me. I'm trying to figure things out, and your patience and understanding mean the world."

Their lips met in a gentle kiss, that quickly deepened as the nerves between them melted away. They spent the night wrapped in each other's arms, the world outside forgotten in the heat of their passion.

The next day, Cassie met Chaz for coffee at a quiet café. Seeing him in person after so long was surreal. His presence was as magnetic as ever, but there was a heaviness in his eyes, a reflection of the time he had spent away. They talked for hours, delving into their shared past and the changes that time had wrought.

"Cassie, I've thought about you a lot over the years," Chaz admitted, his voice tinged with regret. "I never stopped wondering what might have been if things had been different."

She nodded, her heart aching at his words. "I've thought about it too, Chaz. There's a lot we need to figure out, and it's not going to be easy."

They continued their conversation, laying bare their emotions and fears. It was an cathartic experience for both of them, a necessary step in understanding where their relationship stood.

Cassie's interactions with Raphael and Chaz continued, over the next few weeks each encounter bringing new insights and emotions. She found herself torn between the two men, each representing different facets of her cravings and needs. The situation became even more complicated when Raphael almost caught her with Chaz.

Cassie had planned to meet Chaz at a park to discuss some uncleared issues. They sat on a bench near her apartment, the sound of children playing and birds chirping creating a serene backdrop. As they talked, the conversation became more intense, emotions bubbling to the surface.

"I never stopped caring about you, Cassie," Chaz said, his voice filled with emotion. "But I need to know if there's still a place for me in your life."

Before Cassie could respond, she felt a chill run down her spine. She looked up and saw Raphael walking towards them, his expression a mix of confusion and hurt. He had come to surprise her, unaware that she was meeting Chaz.

"Raphael, what are you doing here?" Cassie asked, panic rising in her chest.

"I could ask you the same thing," he replied, his voice tight. "I thought we were supposed to spend the afternoon together."

Chaz stood up, sensing the discomfort. "I should go," he said, looking at Cassie. "We can talk later."

As Chaz walked away, Raphael turned to Cassie, his eyes searching hers. "What's going on, Cassie?"

Cassie responded. "Nothing Raphael just catching up with an old classmate from high school."

Raphael sighed, running a hand through his beard. "When we went to his house why didn't you talk then?"

Cassie reached out, taking his hand. "I care about you, Raphael, but I didn't think it was the right time, barely ever talked and then he left school."

He nodded, though the pain in his eyes was evident. "You should have been honest with me, and he should have too."

The encounter left Cassie reeling, her heart torn between the two men who had become central to her life. She realized that she needed to decide soon, for her sake and theirs.

Cassie spent a lot of time reflecting on her feelings. She visited the places that held memories with both Raphael and Chaz, hoping to find clarity in the echoes of the past. Each memory brought a mix of joy and sorrow, deepening her emotional turmoil.

Arriving back home she sat alone in her apartment, Vanessa called. "Hey, Cassie. How are you holding up?"

Cassie sighed, grateful for the support. "It's been tough, Vanessa. I feel like I'm being pulled in two different directions."

"Remember what I told you," Vanessa said gently. "You need to follow your heart, even if it's difficult. You deserve to be happy, Cassie."

Her friend's words resonated deeply, giving her the strength to face her emotions head-on. Cassie knew she couldn't keep avoiding the decision that loomed over her.

The next morning, Cassie met Raphael for breakfast. She could see the uncertainty in his eyes, a reflection of her own inner demons. While talking, she realized how much he had come to mean to her.

"Raphael, I've been doing a lot of thinking," she began, her voice steady despite the emotions swirling inside her. "I care about you deeply, and I don't want to lose what we have."

His eyes softened, hope flickering in their depths. "I care about you too, Cassie."

They spent the morning together, their bond growing stronger as they shared their hopes and dreams. Cassie felt a sense of peace with Raphael, a feeling that she couldn't ignore.

Later, Cassie met Chaz at their favorite café. The weight of her decision pressed heavily on her, but she knew she needed to be honest with him.

"Chaz, there's something I need to tell you," she said, her voice trembling slightly. "You know I've been spending time with Raphael, and I've realized that my feelings for him are strong."

Chaz's expression remained stoic, though she could see the hurt in his eyes. "I understand, Cassie, but that doesn't change what we have and what you told me while I was away."

Tears welled up in her eyes. "I know, Chaz. You've been an important part of my life, and that won't change. I don't know what to do."

He nodded, reaching out to take her hand. "I appreciate your honesty, Cassie. I hope you find happiness, truly. Let's get out of here and enjoy the rest of the day. No more serious talking, just fun."

Cassie smiled through her tears, grateful for his understanding. They left the café, wandering through the city, living and creating new memories. As the sun began to set, they found themselves in a quiet, secluded park. The atmosphere was serene, and the tension between them started to melt away.

Chaz pulled her close, his eyes searching hers for any hesitation. "Cassie, I know things are complicated, but I still care about you deeply. Let's forget everything for a while and just be in this moment."

Cassie felt a rush of emotions, making her heart race. She nodded, leaning in to kiss him. The kiss quickly deepened, their passion reigniting as if no time had passed.

Without thinking, they moved to a more secluded spot. Their kisses grew more fervent, hands exploring each other with a desperation that had been building for years. The thrill of being out in public only increased their impulses.

Cassie's breath sped up as Chaz's hands roamed under her shirt, caressing her skin. She felt an overwhelming need to be closer to him, to feel every part of him. Chaz seemed to sense this, his own urgency matching hers. He lifted her skirt, his hands skillfully finding their way to the most intimate parts of her.

Their movements became frantic, a dance of passion and longing. Cassie's back pressed against the rough bark of the tree, but the slight discomfort only intensified her arousal. She wrapped her legs around Chaz, pulling him closer, needing him in ways words couldn't express.

Chaz's hands gripped her hips firmly, and he turned her to face the tree. Cassie's hands braced against the bark, the rough texture a sharp contrast to the softness of Chaz's touch. She felt him behind her, his breath hot against her neck as he whispered, "I need you, Cassie."

Her heart pounded in anticipation as she felt him position himself at her entrance. Slowly, he slid into her, filling her completely. Cassie gasped, her head falling back against his shoulder as he began to move. The sensation was overwhelming, each thrust sending waves of pleasure through her body.

The tree's rough bark pressed against her cheek, but the discomfort only heightened her arousal. Chaz's hands moved to her breasts, squeezing them through her shirt, his fingers teasing her nipples. She moaned, the sound muffled by the intensity of their passion.

Their rhythm became more urgent, their bodies moving in perfect sync. Chaz's thrusts grew deeper, each one eliciting a cry of pleasure from Cassie. She felt the orgasm building within her, a coil winding tighter and tighter until it finally snapped.

Cassie's climax hit her with the force of a tidal wave, her body trembling as she screamed with ecstasy. He slid out of her and turned her around putting her on her knees. He followed soon after, his own release shuddering through him as he held the back of her head tightly while shooting his load into the back of her throat. As he pulsed with the tip in the back or her throat she choked.

They stayed like that for a moment, his breathing ragged, hearts pounding in unison. Finally, Chaz gently pulled out of her, standing her up to face him. He kissed her forehead softly, as they shared a moment of post-coital bliss.

They straightened their clothes, Cassie felt a sense of clarity wash over her. The decision ahead was still difficult, but she knew she had experienced something deeply meaningful with Chaz.

Walking back towards the city lights, Cassie knew that this situation became messier. For now, she allowed herself to bask in the warmth of Chaz's presence, knowing that whatever the future held, she had experienced something truly unforgettable.

The next weeks were crucial, Cassie focused on building her relationship with Raphael. They explored the city together, shared countless moments of joy, and faced the challenges that came their way with resilience and love. Their bond deepened, and Cassie found a sense of peace.

Walking along the river, Raphael stopped and turned to her, his eyes filled with love. "Cassie, I know we've had our ups and downs, but I can't imagine my life without you. Will you move in with me?"

Cassie's heart swelled with emotion. She knew that her journey had been fraught with challenges, but she had found her way to a place of love and happiness. "I don't know, Raphael. I know I would love to, but I just don't know right now. Can I think about it?"

Raphael looked slightly disappointed but nodded understandingly. "Of course, Cassie. Take all the time you need. I just want you to be sure and comfortable with whatever decision you make."

Cassie smiled, appreciating his patience. "Thank you, Raphael. It means a lot to me that you understand. I do care about you deeply, and I want to make the right decision for both of us."

They continued their walk, hand in hand, enjoying the tranquility of the evening. Cassie knew she needed to reflect on her feelings and consider the implications of such a big step. She promised herself that she would take the time to sort through her emotions and make a decision that felt right for her heart.

CHAPTER 10

Ten years ago, Chaz would have never thought he would be where he is today. He has a job, three women interested in him, his best friend, and his plan for getting revenge on his brother for everything he put him. Thinking about how life is going now, he decided to just enjoy life and remembered what Raphael and Cassie said when they came to visit him at his place: a double date.

Chaz walked home from work, he felt a sense of hope. The job he found was at a local mechanic shop, which kept him busy and gave him a sense of purpose. He knew the road ahead wouldn't be easy, but he was determined to move forward, one step at a time. Meeting Jenna had given him a new perspective, and the barbecue reminded him that he had people who cared about him.

Chaz decided to call Jenna. They had been texting occasionally, but he wanted to see her again. He dialed her number, feeling a mix of excitement and nervousness.

"Hey, Chaz," Jenna answered, her voice warm and welcoming.

"Hey, Jenna. I was wondering if you wanted to grab dinner sometime this week and have a double date with Raphael and Cassie?" Chaz said, hoping she would say yes.

"That sounds great! How about Friday?" Jenna replied.

"Perfect. I'll reach out to them, and I'll pick you up at seven," Chaz said, a smile spreading across his face.

His plan was to invite Raphael and Cassie and continue to slowly mend the rift between them.

Chaz Called Raphael "Hey, bro, what's up? Got a minute?"

"Sure thing, Chaz. What's on your mind?" Responded Raphael.

"Well, I was thinking, dinner! Jenna and I are planning to hit up that new Italian place downtown this Friday. Thought it might be cool if you and Cassie joined us for a double date. What do you say?" Chaz said with excitement.

Raphael chuckled. "That sounds like a plan, man. Cassie would probably dig that."

Chaz said, "Awesome. I'll text you the details later. Looking forward to it, bro."

"Same here, Chaz. It'll be good to catch up properly." Raphael replied.

Friday arrived, and Chaz found himself looking forward to the double date with Jenna, Cassie, and Raphael. He picked her up and headed to a cozy Italian restaurant. The evening was filled with laughter, good food, and easy conversation. Jenna's presence was an elixir to Chaz's wounded soul, and he found himself feeling lighter and more hopeful.

After everyone had a few drinks, Raphael ordered another round of Smugglers Rhum on the rocks, Jenna noticed the moon shining bright and people started to leave. The four friends—Chaz, Cassie, Jenna, and Raphael—sat around the table. The evening, which had started with laughter and camaraderie, had taken a sharp turn towards discomfort and unease.

Raphael's gaze was intense as he stared at Chaz. "So, you knew all along, huh? That Cassie was in love with you?"

Chaz's jaw clenched visibly. "I didn't think it mattered anymore. It was in the past."

"In the past?" Raphael's voice rose, a mixture of disbelief and anger. "You kept it a secret, Chaz. From me, of all people! How could you?"

Cassie's eyes widened in shock. "Wait, how did you even know, Raphael?"

Raphael's gaze flicked to Cassie. "I found out. Doesn't matter how."

"No, it does matter," Cassie insisted, her voice shaking with a mix of betrayal and confusion. "The only person I told was Vanessa. So, when did you two have time to talk? To my knowledge, you only met once."

Cassie looked at Raphael, her mind racing to put the pieces together. "So, you two were discussing my personal feelings behind my back? When?"

Raphael's face darkened. "Does it really matter when? The point is, I knew, and now everything is out in the open."

Chaz slammed his hand on the table, the sound echoing through the restaurant. "You think you're so righteous, don't you, Raphael? You've been hiding things too."

Raphael stood up, fists clenched. "Oh, yeah? Like what?"

"Like the fact that you're so threatened by me that you couldn't handle knowing Cassie had feelings for someone else," Chaz shot back.

"Enough!" Cassie yelled, standing up and putting herself between the two men. "This is not how we solve this. Secrets are tearing us apart."

Chaz took a deep breath, his eyes softening as he looked at Cassie. "I never meant to hurt you, Cass. I never said anything to anyone. What happened between us stayed between us."

Raphael shook his head, his anger giving way to frustration. "You should've been honest from the start. With both of us."

Cassie looked at them, her heart heavy with the weight of betrayal. "I can't believe this. I thought we were friends. All of us."

Jenna sighed, finally speaking up. "I'm not sure what I got myself into, but this is not what I asked for. This is too much drama for me."

The evening wore on, the four of them sat down again, the animosity slowly giving way to tentative understanding. The restaurant had emptied out, leaving them in a quiet corner, surrounded by the soft glow of candlelight.

Chaz leaned back in his chair, his eyes on Raphael. "How long have you known?"

Raphael hesitated, then sighed. "For a while now. I suspected something, but I didn't know for sure until recently."

Cassie's eyes narrowed. "And how did you find out?"

Raphael glanced at Cassie. "Vanessa mentioned something in passing. It wasn't intentional."

Cassie looked, her voice trembling. "Why didn't she tell me? I'm going to give her a piece of my mind."

Raphael looked down at his hands. "She didn't want to cause any trouble. It slipped out when we were talking, and I thought it was better to let things play out naturally."

Cassie's eyes filled with tears. "I trusted you and her. She was the only one I confided in."

Cassie's voice trembled with hurt and frustration. "So, you knew all this time, Raphael? And you didn't think it was important to tell me? To talk to me about it?"

Raphael sighed heavily, his shoulders tense. "I didn't know how to bring it up, Cass. It's complicated."

"Complicated? You call keeping secrets from me complicated?" Cassie's voice rose, her eyes filling with tears. "I thought we were supposed to be honest with each other, Raphael."

Chaz leaned forward, his voice calm but firm. "Cass, Raphael, let's not do this here. We need to talk about this, but not like this."

Jenna, sensing the escalating aggravation, softly interjected. "Maybe we should all take a breather. Emotions are high right now."

Cassie wiped her tears, her voice shaky. "I can't believe this. After everything..."

Raphael looked torn, his expression pained. "Cassie, I'm sorry. I didn't know how to handle it. I didn't want to hurt you. I should've said something, Cass. I should've told you when I found out you felt that way."

Cassie's shoulders slumped, a mix of anger and sadness in her eyes. "Why didn't you? I thought you wanted me to move in with you. I guess you got your answer."

Chaz hesitated, searching for the right words. "Move in together? You didn't tell me that."

Jenna looked at Chaz with shock and said, "Why does it matter? Why did you invite me here if you obviously have feelings for Cassie?"

Raphael sighed, running a hand through his beard. "Look, can we talk about this somewhere else? This isn't fair to Jenna."

Jenna nodded, her expression compassionate. "Maybe I should just leave it's not like I'm wanted here."

Chaz said shocked and angry, "Look at what you started Raphael because you're a jealous asshole you just caused unnecessary issues in my life and yours. I don't even know why you care who she is or isn't in love with, why don't you tell her your secret."

Jenna stood up and started to walk out before she left, she said, "Raphael lose my number you ruined everyone's night over your jealous bullshit, when she came here with you not Chaz and Chaz before you get involved with anyone else you need to get your house in order. Don't contact me."

Cassie confused about what Chaz just said and replied, "Raphael what is Chaz talking about your secret?"

The waiter came to the table and said, "We are asking you to leave you are causing a disturbance and this is not the establishment for your drama."

Reluctantly, the group agreed to leave the restaurant. Cassie walked out first, her steps heavy with unresolved emotions. Raphael followed, his gaze troubled. Chaz and Jenna exchanged a look before silently following them out.

Outside, in the cool evening air, tensions remained palpable. Cassie stood apart, arms crossed, staring into the distance. Raphael approached her cautiously, his voice gentle. "Cassie..."

Cassie turned to him, her eyes still brimming with tears. "I need some time, Raphael. I need to figure things out."

Raphael nodded, his own emotions raw. "I understand. I just... I didn't want to lose you."

Chaz stood a few feet away, watching them silently. Jenna approached him pulling him to the side, her hand resting lightly on his arm. "I hope you are okay! But I have to end this, I'm sorry but this is too much. I know it wasn't your fault, but I learned a lot today."

Chaz nodded, his gaze still on Cassie and Raphael. "I never wanted this to happen. I just wanted things to be normal again."

Jenna squeezed his arm gently. "Sometimes, things have to get messy before they can get better. They'll figure it out and I hope you do to."

Eventually, they parted ways for the night, each carrying a weight of undecided feelings and unspoken truths. Cassie retreated to her apartment, Raphael to his, Jenna jumped into a cab home in thoughtful silence. Chaz sat in his car evaluating what his next move was. Angry that Raphael started this drama in front of Jenna but hopeful that this just ended him and Cassie.

Days passed with a strained silence between them. Cassie and Raphael spoke sporadically, trying to navigate their emotions and the rift that had formed. Chaz focused on work, throwing himself into his job at the mechanic shop to distract himself from the turmoil within.

Jenna reached out to Cassie. They agreed to meet for coffee, offering a sympathetic ear and gentle advice. Cassie poured out her heart, conflicted between hurt and a desire to salvage whatever relationship they had.

"I'm sorry for what happened the other night." Jenna urged softly. "If he didn't know how to handle what he found out there was a time and place. That wasn't the time and place."

Cassie sighed, stirring her coffee absently. "I know. It's just... hard, you know? I trusted him, and now..."

"I know, that's how I feel about Chaz," Jenna acknowledged gently. "But I wasn't ready for everything that happened the other night."

Chaz, he found himself grappling with the events that transpired. He texted Jessica, seeking her advice.

When she got home, he was able to lay out the situation with a heavy heart.

"I didn't mean for this to happen, Jessica," Chaz admitted, his voice low. "I just wanted things to be normal. I even made it into a double date."

Jessica listened, her expression thoughtful. "Sometimes, honesty comes with a price. But it's the only way to move forward, Chaz."

"I know," Chaz sighed, running a hand up and down his arm.

"You have to give them time," Jessica said softly. "And be ready to accept whatever happens next. In the meantime, you can spend more time with me since Edwin is never around anymore.

CHAPTER 11

Jessica sat in the living room, her mind racing as she heard Edwin's car pull into the driveway. The argument that had been brewing for weeks finally erupted after Edwin noticed that Jessica and his brother Chaz had been in constant contact since Chaz's release from prison. Edwin never wanted Chaz to move in with them, but Jessica had insisted on treating him like family. Now, she had to explain her actions without revealing the truth about her affair with Chaz.

Edwin stormed into the house, slamming the door behind him. His face was flushed with anger, and Jessica could feel the suspense in the air.

"Jessica, we need to talk," Edwin said, his voice barely concealing his rage.

Jessica took a deep breath and nodded, preparing herself for the confrontation.

"Why are you always talking to Chaz?" Edwin demanded. "I never wanted him to move in after he got out of prison, and now it feels like he's always around. What is it?"

Jessica looked at Edwin, her heart pounding. She had to find a way to explain without revealing too much.

"Edwin, he's your brother," Jessica began, trying to keep her voice steady. "He needed support after getting out of prison, and I thought it was the right thing to do. I've been treating him like family, that's all. I told you this already."

Edwin's eyes narrowed. "Treating him like family? It feels like more than that, Jessica. You're always texting him, always talking to him. Why are you so close to him?"

Jessica felt a lump in her throat. She couldn't tell Edwin the truth, not now. Not ever.

"I just wanted to help him adjust," Jessica said, her voice trembling. "He really doesn't have anyone else, Edwin. I thought you'd understand."

Edwin shook his head, his anger not dissipating. "I don't understand, Jessica. I don't understand why you're so involved in his life. He's my brother, but I didn't want him living here because I know the kind of trouble he brings. And now it feels like you're choosing him over me."

Jessica's eyes filled with tears. "I'm not choosing him over you, Edwin. I love you. I just wanted to help him. Why can't you see that?"

Edwin turned away, his shoulders tense. "I don't know what to believe anymore, Jessica. It feels like you're hiding something from me."

Edwin stormed out of the house, Jessica felt a wave of desperation. She needed to talk to someone, and the only person who knew the full story was Chaz. She picked up her phone and called him, but he didn't answer. She sent him a text, hoping he would respond soon.

"Chaz, it's urgent. Please call me when you get this."

Jessica waited, her anxiety growing with each passing minute. Finally, her phone buzzed with a message from Chaz.

"Sorry, Jess. I'm at work. Can't talk right now. What's going on?"

Jessica felt a surge of frustration. She needed to talk to someone, and Chaz wasn't available. In a blind rage, she scrolled through her contacts until she found the number of an old friend. She hadn't seen him in years, but she needed someone to vent to, and he was the only one who came to mind.

Jessica texted Him, asking if he could meet her for drinks. To her surprise, he responded almost immediately.

"Sure, Jess. I'm free tonight. Where do you want to meet?"

Jessica suggested a bar downtown, and they agreed to meet in an hour. As she got ready, she felt a mix of guilt and excitement. She knew this wasn't the best decision, but she needed to talk to someone.

When Jessica arrived at the bar, she spotted him sitting at a table in the corner. He looked older, but still had the same charm.

"Jessica, it's been a while," he said with a smile as she approached the table.

Jessica forced a smile and sat down. "Yeah, it has. Thanks for meeting me on such short notice."

He nodded. "No problem. You sounded upset. What's going on?"

Jessica took a deep breath and began to explain the situation with Edwin and Chaz. She told him about the argument, leaving out the details about her affair with Chaz. As she spoke, she felt a sense of relief. It was good to finally get everything off her chest.

He listened attentively, nodding as she spoke. When she finished, he leaned back in his chair and sighed.

"Sounds like you're in a tough spot, Jess," he said. "But it seems like you're really trying to do the right thing by helping Chaz. Maybe Edwin will come around once he cools down."

Jessica shook her head. "I don't know. It feels like he doesn't trust me anymore. And I can't tell him the whole truth. It would destroy him."

He reached across the table and took her hand. "Hey, you're doing the best you can. Don't be so hard on yourself."

Jessica looked into his eyes and felt a wave of emotion. She hadn't realized how much she missed the comfort of having Him to talk to, someone who understood her.

They continued to talk and drink. The conversation shifted to old times, and Jessica felt herself relaxing. His presence was comforting, and she felt a sense of familiarity with him.

The dimly lit bar was alive with the hum of conversations, the clinking of glasses, and the soft notes of a jazz band playing in the corner. The air was thick with the scent of whiskey and cologne, mingling with the faint aroma of tobacco from a nearby smoking area. At a secluded table in the corner, Jessica and Him sat close, their knees almost touching under the table.

They found themselves laughing and reminiscing about their past. The drinks flowed, and the conversation became more intimate. Jessica felt a spark between them, the same spark that had drawn her to him years ago.

Jessica's eyes flicked to his lips as he spoke, barely registering his words. Her heart was pounding, the alcohol in her system making her bolder, more reckless. She could feel the heat radiating from his body, and the potency of the moment was almost too much to bear.

He stopped mid-sentence, his gaze locking onto hers. The world around them seemed to fade away, leaving just the two of them in a bubble of anticipation. His eyes darkened with lust, and Jessica felt a shiver run down her spine.

Their lips met in a sudden, electric collision. The kiss was intense, filled with an impulsive hunger that had been building between them. Jessica's hands found their way to the back of his neck, her fingers tangled in his hair as she pulled him closer. She could taste the lingering whiskey on his lips, mixing with the sweetness of the cocktail she had been drinking.

He responded with equal fervor, his hands slid up her thigh, pulling her against him. The kiss deepened, becoming more urgent, more consuming. Their mouths moved in perfect sync, tongues exploring, tasting, and teasing. Jessica felt a fire ignite within her, spreading through her body and leaving her breathless.

The noise of the bar seemed to disappear, replaced by the sound of their breathing, the soft moans escaping from their lips. The world outside their kiss ceased to exist; it was just them, lost in a moment of pure, unadulterated passion.

When they finally broke apart, both of them were breathing heavily, their faces flushed. Jessica's eyes fluttered open, meeting his intense gaze. His lips were swollen from the kiss, and she could feel her own heart racing. They sat there for a moment, the air between them charged with unspoken infatuation and the promise of more to come.

The kiss had been more than just an expression of their attraction; it had been a release, a culmination of all the pressure that had been building between them. They sat there, the taste of each other still lingering on their lips, they both knew that things would never be the same again.

They left the bar, their bodies buzzing with the electrifying energy from the kiss they shared. The night air was cool, but the heat between them was undeniable. Jessica's hand found his as they walked, their fingers intertwining in a silent agreement of where the night was heading.

They arrived at his apartment, the door closing behind them with a soft click that seemed to echo with anticipation. The atmosphere inside was intimate, the dim lighting casting shadows that danced on the walls. Without a word, he pulled Jessica close, his lips finding hers once again in a kiss that reignited the fire between them.

His hands roamed over her body, sliding under her shirt to feel the warmth of her skin. Jessica responded eagerly, her fingers deftly unbuttoning his shirt, pushing it off his shoulders. The fabric fell to the floor, forgotten, as they moved towards the bedroom, their movements guided by a shared, unspoken craving.

They stumbled into the bedroom, their kisses growing more urgent. His hands found the hem of Jessica's shirt, lifting it over her head and discarding it. He took a moment to admire her, his eyes dark with desire. "You're beautiful," he whispered, his voice husky.

Jessica felt a thrill run through her at his words, her hands moving to the waistband of his jeans, unbuttoning, and unzipping them with practiced ease. He did the same, his fingers working quickly to divest her of her remaining clothes. In moments, they were both standing naked, their bodies pressed together, the heat of their skin creating a potent mix of sensations.

He guided her to the bed, gently laying her down. He climbed on top of her, his lips trailing kisses down her neck, across her collarbone, and to the swell of her breasts. Jessica moaned softly, her back arching as his mouth found her nipple, sucking and teasing until she was gasping for more.

Jessica's hands explored his body, feeling the tight muscles of his back, the strength in his arms. She pulled him closer, needing to feel him against her. He responded, his kisses moving lower, across her stomach, until he reached the apex of her thighs. He looked up at her, his eyes meeting hers as he kissed her there, his tongue parting her folds and sending waves of pleasure through her body.

Jessica's hands gripped the sheets, her breath coming in short, desperate gasps. His mouth worked magic, his tongue and fingers driving her to the edge and beyond. She cried out, her body shuddering with the force of her orgasm, the pleasure so intense it left her breathless.

He moved back up her body, kissing her deeply, letting her taste herself on his lips. She responded eagerly, her hands finding his erection. She guided him to her entrance, their eyes locking as he pushed inside her, the feeling of him filling her completely making her moan in pleasure.

They moved together in a rhythm that was both urgent and tender, their bodies finding a perfect sync. His hands gripped her hips, pulling her closer with each thrust, driving deeper and deeper into her. Jessica wrapped her legs around him, meeting his movements with her own, their shared pleasure building to a culmination.

Their moans and gasps filled the room, the air thick with the scent of their lovemaking. His thrusts became more erratic, his breathing ragged as he neared his climax. Jessica felt another orgasm building within her, the tension coiling tighter and tighter until it finally snapped, sending her over the edge once again.

He followed moments later, his body shuddering as he spilled into her, the pleasure overwhelming. They clung to each other, riding the waves of their shared release until they were both spent, their bodies slick with sweat, their hearts pounding in unison.

They lay there for a long time, wrapped in each other's arms, the reality of what had just happened slowly sinking in. The intensity of their connection, the depth of their passion, had left them both breathless and wanting more.

As they drifted off to sleep, in each other's arms, the night air outside was cool and still, a stark contrast to the heat and passion they had just shared. The future was uncertain, but in that moment, they were together, and that was all that mattered.

The next morning, Jessica woke up with a pounding headache and a sense of regret. She looked over, he was still asleep and felt a wave of guilt. She knew she had made a mistake, but she couldn't change what had happened.

Quietly, she got dressed and left the apartment, her mind racing with thoughts of what to do next. She knew she had to face Edwin and figure out how to salvage their relationship.

As she drove home, Jessica couldn't help but think about the mess she had created. She had tried to help Chaz, but in the process, she had hurt Edwin and made things even more complicated.

When Jessica got home, Edwin was sitting in the living room, his face a mask of worry and anger.

"Where have you been?" Edwin asked, his voice tense.

Jessica took a deep breath and sat down across from him. "Edwin, I'm sorry. I went out to clear my head."

Edwin looked at her, his eyes filled with pain. "Jessica, I need to know the truth. Why are you so close to Chaz? What's really going on?"

Jessica felt a lump in her throat. She knew she couldn't tell Edwin about her affair with Chaz, but she also couldn't keep lying to him.

"I've been trying to help him, Edwin," Jessica said, her voice trembling. "He needed someone to talk to, and I thought I could be that person. I didn't mean for things to get so problematic."

Edwin shook his head, his eyes filled with tears. "I don't know if I can trust you anymore, Jessica. This whole situation has made me question everything."

Jessica felt her heart breaking. She had made so many mistakes, and now she had to face the consequences.

"Edwin, I love you," Jessica said, her voice breaking. "I never wanted to hurt you. Please, can we find a way to work through this?"

Edwin looked at her, his expression a mix of pain and uncertainty. "I don't know, Jessica. I need time to think."

Jessica knew that her relationship with Edwin was hanging by a thread. She had tried to do the right thing by helping Chaz, but in the process, she had made a series of poor decisions that had only made things worse. Now, she had to figure out how to rebuild the trust that had been broken and find a way to move forward.

CHAPTER 12

Over the next few weeks, Jessica's life descended into chaos. The agitation between her and Edwin was noticeable, every conversation strained and awkward. Edwin's suspicion had turned into quiet resentment, and the emotional distance between them grew wider by the day. Jessica was overwhelmed with guilt and confusion, but she couldn't bring herself to reveal the full extent of her betrayal.

To make matters worse, Jessica began experiencing unsettling symptoms. Morning sickness, strange cravings, and overwhelming exhaustion became her daily reality. She tried to ignore the signs, attributing them to stress and anxiety. But after three weeks of relentless symptoms, she knew she couldn't ignore it any longer.

Jessica made an appointment with her doctor, hoping for some clarity.

Jessica sat in the sterile, white room, her fingers tapping nervously against the armrest of the chair. The sound of the clock ticking on the wall amplified her anxiety.

Finally, the door opened, and Dr. Thompson walked in, holding a clipboard with Jessica's test results.

"Jessica, we've run a series of tests based on your symptoms," Dr. Thompson began, her voice calm and professional. "I have some news for you."

Jessica's heart pounded in her chest. She braced herself for the worst.

"You're pregnant," Dr. Thompson said, looking at her with a mixture of compassion and concern.

Jessica felt the world tilt on its axis. Pregnant? Her mind raced with questions and fears. How was this possible? Who was the father? Was it Edwin, Chaz, or Him? The possibilities swirled around her, each one more daunting than the last.

"Jessica, are you okay?" Dr. Thompson's voice broke through her thoughts.

Jessica managed a nod, though her mind was still reeling. "Yes, I'm just... surprised. Are You Sure?"

"I understand this is a lot to take in," Dr. Thompson said gently. "Yes, I'm sure we ran the test 3 times and you're healthy, and everything looks good so far. Do you have any questions?"

A million questions ran through Jessica's mind, but she couldn't bring herself to voice any of them. "No, not right now. Thank you, Dr. Thompson."

Dr. Thompson nodded. "If you need anything or have any questions, don't hesitate to call. Take care of yourself, Jessica."

Jessica left the clinic in a daze, her mind spinning with the news. She had no idea what to do next.

The days that followed were a blur of confusion and anxiety. Jessica couldn't stop thinking about the pregnancy, but she also couldn't bring herself to tell anyone. Not Edwin, not Chaz, not even Him. She needed time to process everything and figure out what to do.

Edwin noticed her increasing distance and tried to reach out.

"Jessica, you've been so quiet lately. Is something wrong?" he asked one evening, his voice tinged with concern.

Jessica forced a smile. "I'm just tired, Edwin. Work has been stressful."

Edwin didn't look convinced, but he didn't press further. Jessica felt a surge of relief mixed with guilt. She knew she couldn't keep this secret forever, but the thought of revealing it terrified her.

Jessica's mind kept drifting back to that night. The memory of meeting up with Him, his calm presence, the way he had listened to her without a hint of judgment, lingered in her thoughts. She remembered the warmth in his eyes, the gentle way he had reassured her when she felt like her world was crumbling. In that moment, he had been a beacon of solace in the midst of her chaos.

She needed that comfort again, the kind of unspoken understanding that only he seemed capable of providing. As the turmoil of her current situation overwhelmed her, He was the only person who came to mind. Edwin was distant, Chaz was occupied, and He... He was different.

Jessica picked up her phone, her fingers trembling slightly as she scrolled through her contacts until she found Him. She hesitated for a moment, her thumb hovering over the screen. What would she say? How would she explain the mess she found herself in without sounding desperate or pathetic?

She took a deep breath and started typing. "Hey, it's Jessica. We need to talk. When are you free?"

Her heart raced as she stared at the words on the screen. It felt too direct, too vulnerable. What if he couldn't meet? What if he didn't want to? What if...?

Before she could second-guess herself any further, she hastily deleted the message. She felt an ache of frustration, her fingers itching to reach out but her mind pulling her back. She needed to talk to him, but she didn't want to come off as desperate. She needed to phrase it right, find the perfect balance between urgency and casualness.

She tried again, this time with more care. "Hey, you, it's been a while. I could really use someone to talk to. Are you free anytime soon?"

Again, she paused. It still felt too needy, too revealing of her inner confusion. With a sigh, she deleted the message once more. How could she convey the depth of her need without sounding helpless? She closed her eyes, taking a moment to collect her thoughts. She needed to be strong, to find a way to reach out without losing her dignity.

After a long moment of contemplation, she set her phone down, deciding that perhaps she needed more time to find the right words. The last thing she wanted was to rush into this, only to regret it later. She needed to think it through, to make sure she was ready for whatever might come from reaching out to Him.

For now, she would keep her thoughts to herself, searching for the right moment to ask for the support she desperately needed.

Jessica knew she couldn't hide the truth forever. The weight of her secret had become unbearable, gnawing at her every waking moment. She spent a sleepless night turning the situation over in her mind, and by morning, she resolved that it was time to confront Chaz. There was no more delaying the inevitable.

She drove to Chaz's workplace, her heart pounding with each passing mile. Her mind raced with hesitation and fear. How would he react? Would he be angry, shocked, supportive? She parked her car and waited, her fingers drumming nervously on the steering wheel. She had texted him earlier, asking if they could talk during his break, and now all she could do was wait.

When Chaz finally came outside, looking around for her, he spotted Jessica sitting in her car. Surprise flickered across his face as he walked over. "Jessica, what's going on?" he asked, concern evident in his voice.

Jessica took a deep breath, bracing herself for what was to come. "Chaz, I need to talk to you," she said, her voice trembling slightly. "Can we walk?"

Chaz's brow furrowed, but he nodded. "Sure, let's go," he said, gesturing towards a small park nearby. They started walking in silence, the only sound, the crunch of gravel under their feet. The air was thick and Jessica could feel her heart pounding in her chest.

As they walked, Jessica tried to gather her thoughts. She knew this conversation would change everything, but she also knew she couldn't keep the truth from him any longer. She glanced at Chaz, his expression a mixture of curiosity and concern.

Finally, they reached a secluded bench, and Chaz turned to her. "Jessica, you're scaring me. What's wrong?" he asked, his voice gentle but insistent.

Jessica sat down, taking another deep breath. "Chaz, I'm pregnant," she blurted out, her eyes searching his face for a reaction. "And I don't know if you're the father."

Chaz stared at her, his expression shifting from shock to confusion. "Pregnant? But... how? When?" he stammered, struggling to process the news.

Chaz ran a hand through his hair, his mind racing. "Jessica, this is a lot to take in. Are you sure?"

Jessica nodded, tears welling up in her eyes. "I'm sure, Chaz. I've been to the doctor. I don't know what to do. I'm scared."

Chaz sat beside Jessica, his arm wrapped around her shoulders, his mind was a whirlwind of conflicting thoughts and emotions. On the surface, he offered comfort and support, but beneath that facade, a darker realization began to take shape. The goal he had been pursuing for years—the goal of destroying his brother Edwin's life—was unfolding before his very eyes. The revelation of Jessica's pregnancy introduced an element he hadn't anticipated, and he wasn't sure if having a baby was part of the plan.

Chaz's animosity towards Edwin had deep roots. Their rivalry stretched back to childhood, fueled by competition, jealousy, and a series of betrayals that had left Chaz with a simmering resentment. Edwin had always been the golden child, the one who could do no wrong in their parents' eyes, while Chaz had been left to carve out his own path in the shadows. Over the years, that resentment had festered into a deep-seated yearning for revenge.

When Chaz was released from prison, he saw an opportunity to finally turn the tables. He moved in with Edwin under the appearance of needing a place to stay while he got back on his feet. But in reality, he had a plan: to dismantle Edwin's life piece by piece. Seducing Jessica had been a calculated move, a way to get close to Edwin's most vulnerable spot. The affair was meant to be the dagger that pierced Edwin's heart, leaving him betrayed and broken.

Now, as he sat with Jessica, the weight of her revelation settled heavily on him. A baby was a complication he hadn't foreseen. His initial plan hadn't accounted for the possibility of a child, and he found himself grappling with the implications.

On one hand, the pregnancy could be the ultimate blow to Edwin. If the baby turned out to be Chaz's, it would be undeniable proof of Jessica's infidelity and the ultimate betrayal. It would devastate Edwin in a way that nothing else could. But on the other hand, the idea of becoming a father was something Chaz hadn't seriously considered. The responsibility, the commitment, the long-term consequences—it all felt overwhelming.

Chaz's mind raced as he tried to reconcile his conflicting feelings. The hunger for revenge was strong, but so were the doubts. Was he ready to bring an innocent child into this mess? Could he handle the repercussions of his actions, not just for himself, but for Jessica and the baby as well?

Jessica's voice broke through his thoughts, trembling and uncertain. "Chaz, what are we going to do?"

He looked at her, seeing the fear and uncertainty in her eyes. Despite his inner commotion, he knew he had to maintain his composure. "We'll figure this out,

Jess," he said, trying to sound reassuring. "You're not alone in this."

Sitting together in the park, the sun beginning to set, Chaz felt the weight of his decisions pressing down on him. The path ahead was fraught with doubt, and he knew that whatever choices he made would have far-reaching consequences.

For now, he decided to keep his inner conflict to himself. He needed time to think, to plan, and to consider the next steps carefully. The stakes had never been higher, and the future was more uncertain than ever.

EPILOGUE

Time has passed since Chaz had moved in with Edwin and Jessica. Edwin, ever skeptical and resentful of Chaz's presence, often voiced his displeasure through passive-aggressive comments and prolonged absences from home. Jessica, however, remained Chaz's loyal advocate, steadfast in her belief in his potential for change despite the challenges they faced.

Chaz navigated this delicate family dynamic with calculated precision. His efforts did not go unnoticed by Jessica, who appreciated his sincerity and dedication to turning his life around. However, Edwin's distrust and animosity lingered, a barrier Chaz knew he must eventually overcome.

Throughout his journey, Chaz found an unexpected source of support in Raphael, a childhood friend who had reconnected with him during his incarceration. Raphael's unwavering friendship became a pillar of strength for Chaz, reminding him of the genuine connections he had missed during his years of solitude.

Meanwhile, Cassie's letter, confessing her long-standing love for Chaz, caused a flood emotions within him. Seeing Cassie and Raphael together upon his release from prison ignited a thirst within Chaz—a lust not only for Cassie's affection but also to disrupt the bond she shared with Raphael. His determination to create a rift between them stemmed from both a longing for Cassie's love and a deep-seated need to assert control over his fractured life.

Could he reconcile his loyalty to Raphael with the betrayal that had been unveiled? And what did Cassie truly mean to him, now that their connection had been rekindled in such unexpected circumstances?

In a calculated move fueled by unresolved resentment towards Edwin, Chaz embarked on a plan to undermine his brother's marriage. He strategically maneuvered to win Jessica's trust and affection, ultimately leading to an affair that threatened to unravel the fragile peace within the household. For Chaz, it was a form of revenge, a way to inflict upon Edwin the pain and exclusion he had endured during their tumultuous high school years.

With the chaos he wrought, Chaz found a semblance of redemption. The scars of his past, though still present, no longer defined him entirely. His journey from incarceration to integration into his brother's household was a demonstration not just to survival, but to resilience and the transformative power of second chances.

The complexities of Chaz's relationships with Edwin, Jessica, Cassie, and Raphael continued to evolve. The future remained uncertain, fraught with the consequences of his actions and the delicate balance of newfound alliances. Yet, for Chaz, every moment was a chance to rewrite his story, to reclaim his place within the intricate blend of family, friendship, and the pursuit of redemption.

In the thick of the indecision, one thing remained clear: Chaz's journey was far from over. The road ahead was fraught with challenges and revelations, each step a declaration to his resilience and determination to forge a new path.

****

Raphael took Vanessa to dinner on their first official night out together. As they sat at the table, enjoying each other's company, Raphael noticed a familiar face out of the corner of her eye—someone he hadn't seen in years. The woman approached the table and greeted Raphael, "Nice to see you again. It's been a while. Can I have a moment of your time?"

Stepping away from the table, Raphael, frustration evident in his voice, asked, "What are you doing here? Are you following me?" The woman replied, "I'm in town for work, but I knew I needed to see you."

Raphael responded, "Now is not the time. Maybe sometime soon." He walked back to rejoin Vanessa. She asked, "Who was that, and what was that about?"

Raphael replied, "That was Isabella my ex."

Raphael's secrets and the resulting fallout ended, several questions remained unanswered. Raphael's life had been hidden truths and unspoken fears, put together by threads of deception and guilt.

Raphael had always been a complex figure, his charm masking the demons within. His relationship with Isabella, a woman from his past, was a constant reminder of the mistakes he had made. Their history was filled with pain and unsettled emotions, casting a long shadow over his present life.

The revelation of Raphael having secrets sent shockwaves through their circle, especially affecting Cassie and Vanessa. The betrayal cut deep, leaving scars that would take time to heal. Cassie, who had always seen Raphael as a rock in her life, now questioned everything she knew about him.

Raphael's actions had shattered her trust. The question remained: could she ever forgive him, or was their bond unrepairable?

Chaz, too, was caught in the crossfire. His relationship with Raphael had never been complicated. The truth about Raphael's secrets had added a layer of tension to their dynamic, and it was unclear how they would navigate this new reality.

Facing the consequences of his actions, he couldn't help but wonder, would his other secrets stay buried or rise to the surface. The weight of his past mistakes bore heavily on his shoulders, and he grappled with the fear that he was destined to repeat them.

Will Raphael and Isabella ever find closure, or will their past continue to cast a shadow over their lives?

Can Cassie find it in her heart to forgive Raphael, or will she choose to move on without him?

How will Chaz's relationship with Raphael and Cassie evolve when the truth is out?

What other secrets might Raphael be hiding, and how will they impact the lives of those around him?

Can Raphael truly change, or is he destined to repeat the mistakes of his past?

The answers to these questions remained shrouded in mystery, leaving the future uncertain. With everyone grappled with their own emotions and the complexities of their relationships, only time would tell what lay ahead.

****

Cassie had always been drawn to complexity, her own life a testament. Her feelings for Chaz, a man about to be released from prison, had always been a source of internal conflict. She had written him a letter, expressing her long-held love for him, only to receive a response that left her questioning everything.

Chaz's surprise at hearing from her, coupled with his wish that Jessica had told him they were in touch, hinted at deeper layers of emotion and secrecy. Cassie couldn't help but wonder what Chaz's feelings truly were and how their relationship would evolve once he was free.

Adding to her emotional chaos was her complex relationship with Raphael. Cassie had started a relationship with Raphael after writing the letter to Chaz, right before Chaz came home. The affair with Raphael had left her confused with feeling of guilt, passion, and regret.

The revelation of Raphael's secrets had only added to her confusion. As she grappled with the fallout, Cassie couldn't shake the curiosity about a statement Chaz had made to Raphael about a secret he was keeping from her. The mystery gnawed at her, a silent question that demanded answers.

Could she find it in her heart to forgive Raphael, or was their relationship beyond repair? And what did Chaz's secret mean for their future? The questions lingered in the air, unfinished and haunting.

****

Vanessa's journey to success had been a solitary one, her focus persistent, as she built her empire of businesses from the ground up. From her days as a teen event planner to her current role as a lounge owner and entrepreneur, she had dedicated herself wholeheartedly to her work, leaving little time for anything else.

Her involvement in the lives of those around her had always been from a distance, her advice and support given with a sense of detachment. But the recent revelations had forced her to confront her own emotions and the impact of Raphael's betrayal.

Vanessa struggled with the idea of forgiveness. Loyalty was paramount to her, and Raphael's actions had shattered the brick wall around her heart. Will she win his heart? And how would this betrayal affect her relationship with Cassie, who had always looked up to her as a mentor and friend?

As she navigated these complex emotions, Vanessa couldn't help but reflect on her own life choices. Had her relentless focus on success come at the cost of her personal relationships? The questions were as unsettling as they were necessary, and Vanessa knew she had to face them head-on.

✳✳

Jessica stood at the edge of a new beginning, her heart heavy with the weight of her secrets but also filled with a glimmer of hope. She had made mistakes, but she was determined to learn from them and move forward.

Her relationship with Edwin had been a rollercoaster of emotions, the betrayal and subsequent accident leaving them both scarred. Jessica's guilt was a constant companion, a shadow that followed her every step. She had to find a way to make amends, to seek forgiveness not just from Edwin but from herself.

The question of her child's paternity loomed large, a mystery that added another layer of complexity to her life. Who was the true father of her child? The answer was out there, waiting to be discovered, and Jessica was ready to face the truth, no matter how painful.

She looked out over the city, the sun setting in a blaze of orange and pink, she knew that the answers she sought were out there, waiting to be discovered. And with each step she took, she would uncover the truth, piece by piece, until she found the path that would lead her to the happiness, she so desperately craved.

But for now, the questions remained, lingering in the air like a whisper of things yet to come: Would Edwin ever forgive her? Would Chaz find redemption? And who, in the end, was the true father of her child?

Only time would tell, and Jessica was ready to face whatever came next.

****

Edwin had always prided himself on his keen intuition. As a successful attorney, he relied on his ability to read people and situations with precision. Yet, nothing could have prepared him for the gut-wrenching revelation that shook the very foundation of his life.

It began innocuously enough, with small, annoying doubts that crept into his mind like shadows at dusk. Jessica, his fiancée, seemed distant at times, her smiles a little too forced, her excuses for late nights at work a bit too rehearsed. Chaz, his younger brother, was always around—supportive, charming, but there was something in his eyes, a fleeting glance exchanged between them that Edwin couldn't quite decipher.

Then came the whispers. A friend's offhand comment about seeing Jessica with another man at a restaurant, too cozy to be just a friend or family. Edwin dismissed it at first, attributing it to overactive imaginations or jealousy. But the doubts persisted, gnawing at him day and night.

Unable to shake the feeling, Edwin made a decision that would alter the course of his life. He hired Isaac, a discreet private detective known for his meticulousness and discretion. For months, Isaac shadowed Jessica, capturing mundane moments that revealed nothing out of the ordinary. Edwin's anxiety grew, his sleep plagued by restless nights and vivid dreams of betrayal.

One evening, Isaac's surveillance yielded a breakthrough—a meeting between Jessica and someone in a secluded park on the outskirts of town. Edwin watched the footage in stunned silence, his heart sinking with each whispered exchange and stolen touch. His suspicions were confirmed, but the truth was more devastating than he had imagined.

It was his brother Chaz.

With evidence in hand, Edwin wrestled with conflicting emotions—anger, disbelief, and a profound sense of loss. Fury surged through Edwin like a tidal wave. In a moment of reckless abandon, he stormed from Isaac's car, his mind clouded with thoughts of revenge and retribution. Jumping behind the wheel, his vision blurred by tears of betrayal, he sped down the darkened road, unaware of the danger lurking in the shadows.

The crash came suddenly, a sickening symphony of screeching metal and shattering glass. Edwin's world spun into chaos as the impact flung him against the steering wheel, his body broken and battered. Darkness descended, swallowing him whole as unconsciousness claimed him.

About the Author
Tyree Whitworth

Tyree Whitworth, emancipated at the age of 16, has navigated life's challenges independently ever since. Raised by an English teacher who instilled in him a love for storytelling, Tyree discovered his passion for writing early on starting with poetry. His debut novel, Entangled Desires, explores the lessons people encounter in their everyday lives.

At 35, Tyree earned a place on the Part-time Dean's List and was recognized for his academic excellence by being invited into multiple honor societies. He proudly accepted membership in the Phi Theta Kappa Honor Society (PTK).

When not writing, Tyree enjoys playing basketball, coaching youth in his area, and planning ways to give back to the next generation. His diverse experiences, from homelessness to serving 18 months in prison, along with his travels, fuel his intricate and immersive storytelling.

Born in Queens, NY, and raised between Brooklyn, NY, and Maryland. A family nurtured Tyree not his own. He now lives in Long Island with his wife and two sons. Currently, he is working on the sequel to Entangled Desires and a series of children's books inspired by his youngest son.

Connect with Tyree Whitworth on Instagram at @OfficiallyTyree or visit his website at www.Tyreewrites.com for updates and exclusive content.